DEALING WITH THIS THING CALLED COLLEGE

DEALING WITH THIS THING CALLED

COLLEGE

STORIES TO HELP YOU SUCCEED IN UNDERGRAD

CHRISTOPHER SUMLIN

Boyle
&
Dalton

Book Design & Production
Columbus Publishing Lab
www.ColumbusPublishingLab.com

Print ISBN: 978-1-63337-197-2
E-book ISBN: 978-1-63337-198-9

Printed in the United States of America
1 3 5 7 9 10 8 6 4 2

"When you learn, teach. When you get, give."

—Maya Angelou

TABLE OF CONTENTS

DEDICATION

To my beautiful mother, Monica, who sacrificed so much so I could go to college. To you, I owe my life and success. Thank you, Mom.

To my father, ET, who gave me the necessary foundation to complete college with integrity. Thank you for your wisdom. Thank you, Dad.

To my family, friends, and loved ones. Thank you for loving me simply for who I am. For your prayers, well wishes and positive energy. Without you there would be no, THE Chris Sumlin.

I'd also like to thank my good friend Michael McDonald. Mike, we were texting once about my website and blogs and you suggested that I write a body of work that would help students holistically while in college. Your suggestion didn't fall on deaf ears. Thanks for your support.

Lastly, to the great Morehouse College. From the faculty and staff, to the students and alumni, for over 150 years we have built a house founded on brotherhood and black excellence. Thank you to all who came before me, and those who were with me at Morehouse College. Together we worked to create a space where something like me becoming a Morehouse Man was even possible.

FOREWORD

I first met Christopher Sumlin when he was a sophomore at Morehouse College. He started out somewhat reserved, but as he became more familiar and comfortable the real Chris Sumlin slowly made his debut.

In a class full of intelligent young men, Christopher stood out. In addition to having a high IQ, Christopher was hard-working, focused, charismatic, and possessed a machete-sharp wit. Christopher used this wit to become the center of attention in every class. Yet in addition to making all of us laugh and smile, Christopher used his keen intellect and sublime people skills to challenge his classmates to think deeper, bolder, and more independently.

Thanks to a long tradition of Morehouse Men excelling both in front of and behind the camera in Hollywood (Spike Lee; Samuel L. Jackson; Seith Mann; Bill Nunn; Brandon Lawrence; and countless others), entertainment media conglomerates regularly inquire about my best students. These studios, production companies, networks, etc., are constantly looking to hire Morehouse students for internships, and entry-level positions.

When I was contacted by an executive at 20th Century Fox Studios who was looking for an intern to work that summer in Los Angeles, Chris Sumlin immediately came to mind. Based on Chris' stellar work in my Intro to Television class, his strong personal attributes, and his thirst to learn all he could about the entertainment industry, I recommended him for the internship.

After having worked in Hollywood for over a decade, I felt like I knew when someone had what it took to survive and thrive in that sophisticated celluloid jungle. In my opinion, Christopher Sumlin had "*it*." Although I thought Chris indeed had "*it*," what he *didn't* have was a place to stay in Los Angeles for the summer. So we connected with Morehouse alums in the LA area, and true to form, a Morehouse grad arranged for Christopher to have a place to stay while he was interning with 20th Century Fox.

This was all that Chris needed: an opportunity. A shot. He didn't waste it. At the conclusion of his internship in Los Angeles, the studio executives all raved about Christopher. My instincts had been vindicated, and a future mogul in the form of one Christopher Sumlin had emerged.

That successful stint led to another exceptional opportunity for Chris when NBCUniversal asked me who they should hire for their most exclusive and high-profile internship position. I again recommended Christopher, and again he met and exceeded all expectations.

This is Chris' way: he turns lofty dreams into joyous realities. When he envisions a dream scenario, he wakes up from that dream, studies what works, makes a plan, and follows that plan with a focus and determination until his dream becomes his reality.

I couldn't be prouder of Chris. He's a living example of what you can accomplish with the right mindset, and focused actions.

If you read and apply Christopher Sumlin's *Dealing with This Thing Called College: Stories to Help You Succeed in Undergrad*, you will be well on your way to turning your academic and career dreams into your reality, too.

—Adisa Iwa

INTRODUCTION

Dear Reader,

Today is May 22, 2017. The day after my Morehouse College graduation. Wow! I still can't believe it; I'm officially done with undergrad. As I write these very words, I'm faced with a pile of U-Haul boxes that are loaded with the remnants of what I called a life for these past four years at Morehouse. The posters in my dorm have been taken down, a bus ticket has been purchased, and the degree has been earned. It's time for the next chapter.

Today I feel proud and complete. I feel whole for the simple reason that I'm no longer merely Chris Sumlin, but Christopher Michael Sumlin, a Morehouse Man. Yesterday my life changed when I earned a bachelor's degree from the school I had always dreamed of attending. In retrospect, I think I gave my journey here at Morehouse all that I could. I tried my best, I made some excellent friends, and learned invaluable lessons that will stay with me forever. This immaculate journey was an extraordinary one. I'm truly grateful for this experience, but boy, it was far from perfect.

At yesterday's graduation I wasn't recognized as the valedictorian of my class with an impeccable academic track record. I can candidly admit to failing more than a few exams. I failed academic tests, and personal ones as well. There were moments when I lost myself and made decisions that betrayed the very essence of who I am. That sounds heavy, I know, but I can say with confidence that I have no regrets. I wouldn't trade my experience at Morehouse for anything in the world because I know I gave it my all.

There's a Maya Angelou quote that says, "When you know better, you do better." I like to add to that quote and say, "When you know better, you do better, and when you know better, teach others." This mantra is the driving premise of this book.

Dealing with This Thing Called College is a labor of love that I'm hoping will serve as a guide to help you manage college. In this book we will journey together through my college experience; from driving down to Atlanta from Ohio, all the way to commencement. When I was heading to college I looked for how-to books that would give me practical knowledge I could implement to make the college experience less daunting. I also looked for stories that would captivate me and give me insight into what college was really like. I never found that book, so I decided to write it.

I wish I would have had a book like this one when I was graduating from high school. Each chapter consists of a heartfelt, candid story that will give you perspective on my experiences. At the end of each story is a "Ways to Deal" section that provides practical advice. In this book I will discuss academic success, mentorship and so much more. My intention is to share my story as authentically and sincerely as possible. The stories told in this book are chronological, but the lessons are timeless. Feel free to skip around, bounce between chapters and enjoy each moment of reading.

College can be overwhelming and intimidating, I know it was for me. But if there's one thing I know for sure, it's this: if life can bring you to it, you can always get through it. Trust me. You can handle college.

You may be reading this book as an ambitious youngin' looking for insight into college life. Or maybe you're currently in school and want to gain leverage on how to deal with college. You may have come across this book because you want to hear a good story and be inspired. Whatever your reason, I pray this book adds value to your life. The themes, lessons, and stories you're about to read are those anyone can relate to and enjoy.

I ask that you read my story with the understanding that you'll write your own. You're going to have successes, downfalls, and moments that will craft your college experience. Let's just hope that by reading this text your journey may be a tad bit easier, and you'll deal with college even better than I did.

Enjoy this book.

Sincerely,

Chris Sumlin

(1)

THE ROAD TRIP
OF DOUBT

"Cherish your visions and your dreams, as they are the children of your soul, the blueprints of your ultimate achievements."

—Napoleon Hill

I'd like to think that we all have moments of severe doubt. We all have been in situations that make us question our intelligence, our worth, our abilities. We may overestimate a situation and underestimate ourselves. Unfortunately, I had a moment like this on my way to college.

It was a rainy day in August of 2013. My family and I packed up all my belongings and headed toward Atlanta and Morehouse. My father was driving, and as I sat in the seat behind him I was overwhelmed with anxiety. Tears filled my eyes as thoughts of my journey through high school ran through my mind. I'm not sure what poured more, the clouds of rain that saturated the skies over the interstate roads, or the tears flowing from my eyes. I had a real moment when I realized I was starting a journey that would change the trajectory of my life forever. You'd think that I would be excited and ecstatic to be heading to college, but the only thing running through my head was doubt.

For me, college was uncharted territory. As a young man growing up in Columbus, Ohio, I never met anyone who had graduated from Morehouse. I could count on one hand the number of family members who had earned bachelor's degrees. I wondered how going off to college would change me and life as I knew it. I pondered, *What is Morehouse going to be like for me? How is this school going to help me grow? Who will my friends be? Will I be liked?* This road trip seemed endless.

On top of my doubts and insecurities, I reflected on the people who were against my decision to attend Morehouse. The backlash I faced from announcing I was going to Morehouse affected me deeply. During my last few weeks of high school, I was overwhelmed with love and support daily. I went to an early college high school that allowed me to take college courses. This early college program granted me access to classes at Ohio Dominican University. I started taking classes at sixteen, and by nineteen I had enough credits to earn an associate of arts degree.

This degree was an accomplishment, and something that I was proud of, but I knew it was easy to obtain because of the support within my program. The class routine was easy to manage. Each day I would check in with my high school teachers, take a class at ODU, and return to my high school with my peers. I still lived with my parents, stayed close with all my friends, and was technically still a high school student. Once I understood that I would walk in the ODU commencement exercise, I knew that I wanted more than an associate degree. I felt strongly that if I worked hard on my applications, then maybe I could go to a four-year institution and earn my bachelor's. The odds were stacked against me. I had a twenty on the ACT, mediocre grades, and no idea how the collegiate admissions process worked, but I believed.

With faith, hard work and research I applied to nine schools. These were schools that I found on Google and ones close to home. As a high-schooler I had this vision of myself going to classes, living independently, and getting out of Columbus. I applied to Baldwin Wallace University, the University of Dayton and other liberal arts schools. I also entertained the idea of going to a HBCU (historically black college/university), so I applied to Morehouse and Howard. During the spring of my last year of high school, I got accepted into all nine schools to which I had sent applications. Everyone was so proud that I had followed my vision and believed in myself enough to apply. Getting accepted felt like winning the lottery.

The acceptance letters started rolling in, and the financial aid packages soon followed. By this stage in my college admissions process it was time to decide where I would officially enroll. I knew that it was a blessing to get accepted, but honestly I had no method for how I came up with these nine schools. The colleges just came to me on a whim through Google searches, or were schools I had heard that my teachers had attended. Following my acceptances, I began intensely researching each school and their alumni. My mom thought Baldwin Wallace was an excellent choice because it was close to home and they awarded me a near full ride. My father wanted me to go to Morehouse since it was a HBCU, and he had dreamed of going there as a young man. Many of my peers at my high school thought it would be safe for me to continue my time at Ohio Dominican and study there. I can't lie, Ohio Dominican was a strong option because I would have paid next to nothing to attend; the financial aid package they gave me was by far the best of my nine schools.

I looked into each college and weighed everyone's opinion, but once I did my research on Morehouse, I knew that was where I wanted to go. I saw videos of young black men dressed in white shirts and maroon ties; I read articles on Dr. Martin Luther King and Dr. Benjamin Elijah Mays. As I saw photos of students at Morehouse, I envisioned myself as a student there and it felt right. I told my parents, "Morehouse is where I belong." That was it, and the decision was final.

Unfortunately, of all the schools I was accepted to, Morehouse awarded me the least financial aid. Of course, my family wasn't too pleased to hear this news. The love and support that I felt for getting accepted into these colleges instantly transformed to fear and concern.

"Morehouse is a good school, but it's costly, how are you gonna pay for it?"

"You don't know anyone in Atlanta, how do you expect to get around?"

"Do you think you have what it takes to go to that school?"

"Morehouse may be too good for you."

These were the sentiments I seemed to hear continually. I understood what my loved ones were trying to bring to my attention. They were trying to get me to think rationally and appropriately weigh the decision.

Morehouse was uncharted territory. I had never met anyone with first-hand experience of Morehouse, so there was no one I could call up to ask about the school. The only thing I knew for sure about Morehouse was that I belonged there. I had a clear vision in my mind as to what my life would look like going to school in Atlanta, and I believed in it.

I trusted this vision and began to articulate it strongly to those around me. Eventually, my mother knew my mind was made up, and together we did all the paperwork to make sure I was going to Morehouse. Mom took out loans, Dad believed I was making a sound decision, and I had the vision. Together, my family and I did everything in our power. Before I knew it, we were on the road headed down to Georgia.

As I sat there on the road to Atlanta, I reflected on the negative feedback I had received. My vision for myself had begun to fade. My confidence was subsiding. All I could think of was the negativity, my doubt, and insecurities. As we drove down the highway, the feelings that struck me the hardest stemmed from the realization that the discouraging advice I was getting wasn't coming from haters or people who didn't know me. The words of "wisdom" advising me not to go to Morehouse came from those I loved. These were people I cared about, and with whom I had shared profound moments. These people were my family, close friends, and high school teachers I'd admired. I didn't understand how the majority of these people didn't seem to understand or believe in the vision I had for myself. I thought that I had proven my ability to make things happen.

I said to myself, *Am I not the man who graduated from Ohio Dominican University with an associate degree at nineteen? Am I not the guy who has a work ethic good enough for college? How can anyone who knows me not believe in my ability to go to Morehouse and make it happen?*

I was terrified. I honestly didn't know what to do. Fortunately, by the time I felt this fear, it was too late to run. I was already packed up, my semester had been paid for, and it was time to start the journey I had envisioned.

After hours of reflection, my family and I made it to Morehouse campus. When we finally pulled up to my dorm in the W. E. B. Du Bois International House, I was still a little nervous.

"All right, go ahead and unload your stuff," my father said as he popped open the back of the truck.

My heart sank, I stepped out of the truck and went to the back to grab my luggage. As I grabbed my first item, I was approached by some upperclassmen.

"Hello, Brother, welcome to Morehouse. Do you need some help?"

I was shocked. I stood there, barely understanding what was happening. In mere seconds, four Morehouse guys were helping me take my belongings into the building. I had read online how Morehouse was known for its camaraderie and brotherhood, and at that moment, as an incoming freshman, I experienced it first-hand.

Dad stayed in the truck and watched with contentment as my sister Britney, my mom and I went to my assigned dorm room, room 408. When I opened the door, it was as if I were opening the doors to Narnia—an uncharted land of opportunity. I understood that this was the place where I would spend my first year in college. Shortly after I was all settled in, my sister and mother left. I walked around the hall where I met my dormmates on my floor. As I interacted with each brother on my floor, I realized we were all the same. We all had visions of what we wanted for ourselves and how

Morehouse was going to help us all get there. It was at this moment that I knew I had made the right decision.

Looking back, I think the big lesson to learn from this moment is the importance of sticking to the vision. Roy T. Bennett writes in his book, *The Light in the Heart*:

> *Don't let others tell you what you can't do. Don't let the limitations of others limit your vision. If you can remove your self-doubt and believe in yourself, you can achieve what you never thought possible.*

Vision is so hard to maintain in the face of adversity. I believe that life has a way of talking to all of us and giving us insights. I knew that life was speaking to me when it said that Morehouse was where I was supposed to be. The vision came to me the day I held the brochure in my hand. Shannon Taylor, one of my high school counselors, gave me the brochure when she suggested I look into HBCUs. The vision was given to me again when I watched videos about Morehouse on YouTube. It was a feeling I couldn't explain, but I could just see myself in one of those white button-ups with the maroon tie. I saw the vision in my heart clear as day. Those around me may not have supported it, but the vision wasn't given to them, it was given to me.

As you start any journey, you will have personal ideas and visions. Images of what you want to accomplish and who you want to be. I believe there are two types of visions that a person can experience. One type of vision you may have is a premeditated vision. The premeditated vision-making process may consist of making vision boards, writing down a goal list, or deciding what you want to accomplish. My goal was to go to a four-year school and reach for a bachelor's degree.

The second type of vision I believe we have are those visions that life gives us. These can come as dreams one may experience in sleep, through a conversation that may transpire with another person, or a strong sense of intuition. Some people may refer to these visions as "life," "The Universe," "my gut," or "intuition." I call them God—God's way of speaking to all of us. These kinds of visions are unexplainable and instinctive. Growing up we used to watch lots of Bible-based movies. In these films, biblical characters like Moses and Noah always heard from God through this great, deep voice throughout their journey. I think that the "great, deep voice" only comes in the movies. I've come to understand that life has a way of talking to us through our feelings, inclinations, and thoughts. That's the vision formation.

In today's society we often hear people talk down to visionaries.

"Oh you're such a dreamer."

If someone were to call me a dreamer, I would rearticulate it as being a visionary. When we deny ourselves our visions, we deny ourselves the possibility of expressing the truth of who life

9

may be calling us to be. This notion of ignoring a vision is dangerous and counterintuitive to living the life of our dreams. In my experience, both positive and negative visions have led me to make some of my best decisions. When my dreams are too big for some to conceive, it's the positive images from my envisioning practice that keep me going.

When I was a young boy and my parents would take us clothes shopping, my siblings and I were always instructed to try on the clothes before my parents would buy them. In theory, the pants or shirt may be the right color, size, and brand, but it wasn't until we wore the clothes and they felt right that my parents would buy them.

I remember asking myself questions in the mirror before I ever asked my parents to buy me anything: "Can I see myself wearing this? What can I see myself wearing this with?"

In retrospect, I was asking myself what vision I had for that purchase. Do your best to be a visionary. When you don't know what to do next, do nothing. Wait for the vision to come, and once you get a vision or a goal, look within yourself for instruction. For me, the vision was going to college; I knew that to follow through with that vision I had to decide to work hard and apply to those colleges. I can't even fathom how different my life would be had I not followed my vision of attending Morehouse. I do know that I would have regretted it. Who wants to live life with regrets?

Oprah Winfrey didn't let others tear her from her vision. Oprah often tells the story of the crossroads she faced while in college. During her college career at Tennessee State University, she was given an opportunity to work at a news station in Nashville. She was faced with the decision of either leaving school or pursuing a new venture as a news anchor. Oprah recounts that she was unsure whether to take the job or not. Her art teacher, Mr. Cox, told her that it was a good idea worth entertaining.

Soon after that conversation with Mr. Cox, nineteen-year-old Oprah was hired to work in television as a news anchor in Nashville. During her time as a news anchor, Oprah said that she could "feel inside herself" that news anchoring wasn't the right thing for her. This moment was when Oprah was given the vision, and it was a strong gut feeling. She was offered a job in Atlanta with a $40,000 salary but refused to take it because she could *feel inside herself* that she wasn't ready. During a talk at the Stanford Graduate School of Business Oprah stated, "I started listening to what felt like the truth for me."

A couple of years later she moved to Baltimore and was a news reporter making $22,000 a year as a twenty-two-year-old. It was here that Oprah again felt that reporting was not for her. Unfortunately, everyone around her was telling her that it was a good move because of the money she was making. In this moment Oprah had the choice to resist the vision she had for herself or listen to the opposing advice of her friends and family. Instead of staying in news anchoring, Oprah was demoted to a talk show and asked to interview a local ice-cream man about ice-cream flavors. It was here that Oprah found a home for herself as a talk show host.

Oprah credits the start of her journey to that decision to stay in Baltimore instead of taking the job in Atlanta for the $40,000 salary. She decided to stay in Baltimore through the late 1970s and work there because it felt right for her. That vision of staying in Baltimore led to her working on a talk show in 1978 entitled *People Are Talking*. This job in Baltimore led her to another opportunity in Chicago. The job she took at the Chicago station was a morning talk show called *AM Chicago*, which inevitably became *The Oprah Winfrey Show* in 1986. The rest is history.

Would Oprah have become the billionaire media mogul she is today had she taken the job in Atlanta? We will never know. But we do know what happened to Oprah when she believed in her vision for herself.

It's so important that we honor the visions we receive in life. As you leave high school, so many opportunities may come your way, and you may not know what to do next. I encourage you to envision the best move for your life. Do your research, visit campuses, and talk to current students at the institutions you wish to attend. After you weigh your options, find what feels right for you. After my college research, Morehouse felt right to me. You may face opposition, and that is OK. Remind yourself that the vision is for you. Remember to be aware that just because something feels right to you, doesn't mean that it will please everyone else.

It's imperative that you understand that your visions and feelings must come from you. People love living vicariously through others and projecting their desires on everyone but themselves. I'm a big Beyoncé fan, and each time Beyoncé has a big performance there are always those individuals who feel like she should perform this or that. In sports, there are always fans in the stands who feel like they can call the plays better than the coach. In your life, you're Beyoncé with a big performance. You're the coach with the Super Bowl play in the last few seconds of the quarter. Inevitably, no matter who tries to advise you or not, you are the one who has to endure the consequences of your decisions. It will be you walking across that stage at commencement at the end of your college experience with a degree in hand.

A lot of people didn't see it for me when I told them I wanted to go to Morehouse, but I made it and graduated. Many people didn't see it for Oprah and wanted to direct her career as a news anchor, but she didn't let them. Always remember to honor your visions no matter who is against you.

When you arrive at school, there may be a major that you desire to pursue that your parents may not support. There might even be a fraternity or sorority that you want to join against the counsel of your friends. You know what to do whenever you face a tough decision.

First, get in your feelings. Visualize and see yourself flowing in your vision. Does this visualization make you feel good? Excited? Passionate? If the answer is yes, then drown out all the excessive noise from those who say you can't do it. Viola Davis said, "The greatest joy of a lifetime is having the honor of being who you truly are." See your visions and manifest them no matter what.

I can say with certainty that when you manifest your goals against the counsel of others, that alone is the best feeling. As you start your college journey keep the visions and plans you have for yourself and make them happen, you deserve it.

WAYS TO DEAL

When Working on College Applications

- Read lots of books when writing your admissions essays
  - Great writers are good readers.

- Get involved in your community
  - Community service looks fantastic on a college application.

- Make sure your letters of recommendation are by individuals who can speak not only to your professional performance, but also to your character
- Ask for application fee waivers
  - Certain schools have application fees that can be very expensive. Make it a priority to ask for fee waivers for each of your applications.
  - Application waivers aren't a guarantee, but it is a good choice to try and ask.

- Be honest on every part of the application
  - The truth always reveals itself in these kinds of processes, so always be honest.
  - With your accolades, grades and essays, always tell the truth.

- If you get deferred from a college don't give up
  - Send emails to the school and respectfully advocate for your admission.
  - Ask questions about your application and follow up with admissions recruiters.
  - Don't be afraid to send LinkedIn messages or emails discussing your application.

When Traveling to College

- Drive to college rather than fly
  - You can take more items in a truck than on an airplane.

- Pack lots of underwear but few clothes
  - Your style in college will change from what you wore in high school. Don't over pack—a lot of the clothes you wore in high school you won't wear in college.

- Look online for lists of college essentials
  - Most schools provide a shopping list for incoming freshmen that tells you what to bring to school. Look for this list and buy what you can.

When Trying to Get Visions for Your Life

- Spend time alone
  - ○ Do a lot of research, watch new things, and journal ways to make big changes in your life.

- Talk to people you admire
  - ○ Self-reflection and alone time is good, but after that, conversing with someone you look up to can help organize your thoughts and your next big move.

- Create vision boards
  - ○ Whether electronic or physical, vision boards are a big way to help manifest your future.

- Ignore "dream killers"
  - ○ Dream killer: someone who will find any reason to tell you that you can't do something.
  - ○ Constructive criticism that is well intended is awesome, but dream killers are not. Avoid dream killers at all costs.

MAYA

"A mind is like a parachute. It doesn't work if it is not open."

—Frank Zappa

As you navigate through college you will experience a lot of new people and ideas. The individuals you meet may have different perspectives, come from different lifestyles, and/or be unlike anyone you have ever met before. When I started my college experience I had a linear view of what I expected people to be like at Morehouse, and what their lives would be. I had a narrow view of how I predicted I would make friends, and who I would spend my time with. Within my first days of college, my predictions and closed views were soon shattered.

I was always told that college will be where you find your friends for life. During my first days of walking the campus of Morehouse, I was always wandering around wondering who would become my "friend for life." I was a man on a mission;

always smiling, adding to conversations where I could, and leaving my dorm room door open. I had a high school teacher named Jane Hatch who told me if I left my dorm room door open I would surely make friends. I had a fun time testing this theory daily. My floormates would come in, they would see my snacks, ask to have some, and then shortly leave. I was never discouraged. We had all just settled into our rooms, and I knew that I'd find a Morehouse brother to bond with sooner or later. I didn't have much luck during the first few days I was at Morehouse, but little did I know, it would be a Spelman student who would soon become my best friend.

At Morehouse we had New Student Orientation. NSO, as it's commonly referred to, is a time of celebration and tradition as the college welcomes its newest students. I had no idea what was in store for me during that first week, and boy was I in for an unforgettable experience. I got to witness programs, learn about the school's history, and meet Morehouse alumni whose impact would change my life. Of all the events taking place that week, all my dormmates kept talking about the Morehouse-Spelman brother/sister exchange. This event was one of the final events of NSO and was set to take place that Sunday.

I had heard upperclassmen reference their Spelman sisters before in passing, but I never knew how I was supposed to get one. After asking around, I learned that this was an exchange program—each Morehouse student was paired with a Spelman student to help the two navigate the Atlanta University Center.

Morehouse, the all-male institution, is located on Westview Drive. Directly across the street is Spelman College, the all-female institution. There are multiple colleges all within blocks of each other, such as: Morehouse, Spelman, Clark Atlanta University and others. Together these schools make up the Atlanta University Center, often referred to as the AUC.

I heard stories about guys who would have their sisters bring them medicine when they were sick and go to church with them on Sundays. Brothers I conversed with shared stories of how their Spelman sisters went to brunch with them and many other fun activities. All of the conversations I heard were about the bond that is built between a Man of Morehouse and his Spelman sister. I was excited as I knew that this was my chance to meet the best friend I had yearned to have.

The night before the exchange, all of us first-year Morehouse students were discussing what we wanted our relationships to be like with our Spelman sisters. We were all so excited to discover what it was going to be like meeting them, and what our bonds with our sisters would be like. Some guys wanted a Spelman sister who was pretty, and others wanted a young lady they could go to church with, etc. I just knew that I wanted my Spelman sister to be...well, nice.

During my first days at Morehouse, I was terrified of Spelman. I had this big fear that my Spelman sister would be mean or not want me to be her Morehouse brother. Of course, Morehouse is a historically black, all-male institution, known for producing influential black leaders. Spelman, across the road, is demographically the same institution, but for black women. I was very familiar with the grandeur of Morehouse Men, and was proud to know I was part of its legacy. Conversely, I was petrified of the kinds of women I was in store to meet over at Spelman, because I knew they were just as great, if not greater than Morehouse guys.

That night I told my Morehouse brothers that I just wanted my Spelman sister to be kind and to like me. That evening I tried my best to iron my clothes and choose a cologne. My mother always told me that women love a good-smelling man. I had some AXE that had caught the attention of the women at my former job, so I figured maybe it would work on my future Spelman sister. With my ironed outfit, and cologne ready for the next day, I said a prayer asking that I would get a Spelman sister, and she would be the best friend of my dreams.

The next day, the morning of the exchange, my residential advisor told us all to line up and prepare to head over to the chapel where we would meet our Spelman sisters. As we waited in line, the team of RAs sold us pink flowers that we could give as gifts to our newly-introduced sisters.

"Make the ladies feel special and buy them flowers, brothers," the RA said.

Some guys bought none, while others bought one. I bought three.

I thought, *My Spelman sister will love me because I bought her three flowers.*

I was all ready to go. I remember taking a picture with my flowers and a smile, anticipating what was to come. I had my flowers, I was all lined up and headed to King Chapel for convocation.

NSO convocation was pretty good. I remember all of us Morehouse brothers walking up to the chapel. I saw this long line of the most beautiful women I had ever seen. The Spelman freshmen were all lined up, beautifully dressed and smiling. I was fascinated that all of them were wearing white dresses. I wondered why they couldn't have told all of us guys to wear black suits or some other matching clothing. The girls beat us to the chapel, and they were lined up so neatly. On the other hand, guys were all over the place. Some guys' shoes didn't match their belts, shirts weren't tucked in, and some brothers didn't even bother to iron. I instantly got nervous again. Before I knew it, we were seated in convocation, and the program had begun.

After Sunday morning convocation it was time for the moment I had been waiting for—time to meet my Spelman sister. By this point one of my flowers was bent up because I had been holding it too tight. I tossed it, put a smile on my face and headed out to the line to meet my sister.

All of the freshmen at Spelman were on one side of the chapel, and all of the freshmen from Morehouse were on the other. There was a path that led each student to the center of the chapel at a midpoint. One Morehouse student would come from the left, and a Spelman student from the right. Whoever you met at the midpoint was your "Spelhouse" sibling—a term used to describe Morehouse and Spelman as one. When I made it to the meeting place, there she was. We instantly locked eyes, locked arms, and walked away from the chapel as a new pair of Spelhouse siblings.

"Hi, I'm Maya," she said to me in the sweetest voice, like a friend I had known my entire life.

As I looked into her eyes, I could see that she wanted me to like her just as much as I wanted her to like me.

"Hi, Maya. I'm Chris from Ohio."

I gave her two pink roses, we exchanged social media accounts and hugged. This minute was the beginning of a friendship that would last for years to come.

In the months following our initial meeting, Maya and I hit it off. We went to the mall together, she introduced me to her friends, and always helped me navigate Spelman when I would visit the campus.

Later in my freshman year, many of my dormmates said that they no longer talked to their Spelman sisters. On the other hand, Maya and I stayed in touch and looked out for one another. She truly became the best friend I had dreamed of meeting while in college.

The lesson I learned from this experience was the importance of an open mind. When my Morehouse brothers and I heard of the Morehouse-Spelman sibling exchange, some guys were so closed-minded about what they wanted their Spelman sisters to be. They had their lists, their demands, and expectations of what they wanted. I only wanted my Spelman sister to be a kind girl; my mind was open to whoever she might have been.

Luckily, my Spelman sister Maya is phenomenal. To this day we are still friends and very close. We have our similarities, and we have our differences, but we still love each other fully. I can't say where our relationship as Spelhouse siblings would be if I had approached her with preconceived notions about who she should be. This idea of having an open mind in regard to relationships helped me meet a lot of great friends during my time at Morehouse.

College is a time of self-exploration and discovery. No matter where you go to school, you will meet people from all different walks of life and backgrounds. Be open to meeting friendly people. If you can find individuals who respect you and treat you right, do your best to honor them with an open mind and accept them for who they are. I can say with confidence that having an open mind will allow you to meet some of the best people ever.

There were a number of instances in college when I met someone who shared a different political view than I held, or who maybe didn't think Beyoncé was the best entertainer in the world, but we still connected. You will grow immensely during your time in college, and an open mind lays the foundation for you to do so.

Whether a person is a different ethnicity, has less or more money than you, or whatever the differentiating factor may be, keep an open heart. No matter what kind of ideas or views he or she shares, do your best to have an open mind.

Be nice, be smart, but be open-minded.

WAYS TO DEAL

When Meeting Someone for the First Time

- Be yourself
  - People can spot a phony a mile away. When you meet someone for the first time don't be afraid to let your hair down and be yourself.
  - Don't try to be the person you think others want to meet—just be yourself. You are enough.
- Be mindful of your hygiene
  - No one forgets bad breath or body odor. It should go without saying that personal hygiene is always a priority, but people forget. Practice good hygiene.
  - Whenever I'm in a situation where I will be expected to talk to people in close proximities I always have

    Tic Tacs or breath strips on standby to keep my breath smelling fresh.

- ○ Deodorants and mints are **complements** not substitutes.

- Suspend judgment
  - ○ People are complex and multi-layered. Never think you know someone well after just one impression. Take a moment to get to know the person deeply before concluding anything about him or her.

When in Conversations with A New Person

- Listen more than you talk
  - ○ We all love talking about ourselves, and it is easy to take over conversations when meeting someone for the first time. Make it a point to listen more than you talk, and your friends will love you a lot more.

- Treat people like a loved one
  - ○ Would you go to a loved one, interrupt his/her conversation, exchange Snapchats, talk about yourself and then walk away? Heck no. Treat relationships as you'd treat your friendships. Build rapport and trust as early as possible.

- Get invested
  - ○ Keep good eye contact with the person you are meeting.

○ Put your phone away when someone is talking to you unless it is directly appropriate and you are sharing the screen with him or her. Having your phone in anyone's face for any reason is just plain rude.

○ Tilt your body toward the person speaking and nod your head along with what they are saying. These small cues go a long way when making people feel important and showing them you care.

When the Relationship Starts to Form

● Reciprocate effort

○ If someone is making the effort to reach out to you, try and respond. Everyone is busy but make it a point to choose people who choose you.

● Don't overshare

○ In her book *Daring Greatly,* Dr. Brené Brown discusses the difference in being authentic and oversharing. She teaches that authentic people build relationships over time, but oversharers blurt out extremely personal information in an attempt to gain a hot-wired sense of intimacy without the prerequisite of being trustworthy.

● Honor people by remembering small details

○ Whenever people share small details about themselves or their families, make an effort to remember this information. This shows you care.

○ Recollecting small details about a person is hard at first, so when small information presents itself make it a point to jot it down on paper when you're alone so you'll remember later.

3

TRY AGAIN

"Our greatest weakness lies in giving up. The most certain way to succeed is always to try just one more time."

—Thomas A. Edison

Failure can be defined as a lack of success. Many people try to avoid the mention of failure and feel that it is something that should be hidden. We have all experienced failure. It is an inevitable part of life. Not everyone may be blessed to experience success, but all of us have experienced some form of failure. A truth that I have come to accept is this—if you plan to do anything of value, you can anticipate failure's ugly head looming at some point in time. This shared feeling of failure is something we can all relate to, but many of us differ significantly when it comes to our reactions to failure.

I have been through many failures and tough times. I've been a part of failing relationships, failed tests, and have even failed classes. What I have tried to emphasize in my life is how I respond to my failures. My grandmother used to tell me, "Life is ten percent what happens to you and ninety percent how you respond to it." This notion of responding to failure positively can serve us all.

The story of how I met the singer Ashanti is a testament to this idea. At this point in my college journey I was all settled into classes. My parents had made it safely back to Ohio, I was in my dorm, and the journey had officially begun. One evening I was walking through campus and spotted a friend named Daniel Flack. Flack, as I called him, was a real cool guy. I followed him on Instagram during the summer before starting Morehouse. We had moments where we sat in the cafeteria together and shared good conversation about music, fashion, and most notably, Kanye West. I enjoyed talking with Flack because he always said what was on his mind and never cared what anyone thought about it. As I ran into Flack that evening, he was in a frenzy.

"Hey, what's up, Chris? I got to go I'm headed to an audition," he said quickly.

"Where to? Who's on campus? What's about to happen?" I replied.

He told me he was going to audition to be part of the glee club. My brother Orlando was in the glee club during his time in college. When I heard that Flack was going, I decided to tag along. Luckily, I made the glee club as a first tenor in the second choir. I loved being in the glee club; being a member of such a talented group gave me purpose and helped me navigate campus easier.

After a few weeks of rehearsal, we had our first performance. The performance was to commemorate Ray Charles and honor him with a US postage stamp. When I found out that I was going to be a part of this monumental event I was ecstatic. I got my glee club blazer nice and pressed, shined my shoes and was ready to sing my heart out.

The morning of the performance was hectic. I woke up behind schedule and was late to the call time. As I walked to glee club, I was shaking because I was so ashamed of my tardiness and what everyone would think of me being the "late freshman." The glee club upperclassmen were disappointed with me because I was late. I tried to dip into the line with my fellow first tenors, but that didn't work. As I tried to make my way to what I thought would be my place in line, I was pulled to the side by one of the glee club seniors.

"Sumlin, you're late, and you're not in dress code."

By this time the entire glee club was looking over at me to see what was happening. Mortified would be an understatement to describe how I was feeling. I thought to myself, *How can I be out of uniform?* When I looked down at my pants there was a big difference from what I had on compared to everyone else. I wore black slacks with my glee club attire instead of the grey slacks that everyone else was wearing. Not only was I late, embarrassed, and sweating bullets, but I was also out of uniform.

Overwhelmed with shame, I went to discuss what had happened with our director. At this time Dr. David Morrow had been the director of the Morehouse College Glee Club for over twenty years. Dr. Morrow was a Morehouse Man and was the valedictorian of his class. His standards of excellence and high expectations are what keep the glee club thriving to this day. When I knew I was going to disappoint him, I was petrified. Dr. Morrow probably didn't know my name, and after this he would likely remember me as "the late freshman."

Fortunately, Dr. Morrow was a lot nicer than I expected. I think he could feel the shame and disappointment I was feeling. I also think he had some mercy when conversing with me because I was a freshman.

"Sumlin, it's all right. You didn't know," Dr. Morrow said. After he said those words it was like a weight had been lifted from my shoulders. Not only was Dr. Morrow kind and caring, he also knew my last name.

"Thanks, Dr. Morrow. I apologize," I said calmly.

"Next time ask if you aren't sure about something. I'll see you in rehearsal this evening."

I guess that was a pleasant way of saying, you're still in the glee club, you just aren't singing with us today. I pleasantly smiled, assured him it wouldn't happen again, and left the concert hall.

As I walked out with my sweaty face, shame, and black slacks, I was hurt. I went to go vent to someone who would listen and reassure me that I didn't just make the biggest mistake of my life.

I walked to the office of Dr. Elania Hudson. Dr. Hudson is a great mentor and had been mentoring me since I started at Morehouse. I knew she would know what to say. I walked into her office fresh from the most embarrassing moment ever.

"Hello, Mr. Sumlin. How are you, superstar?" she asked.

I told her the entire situation and how I felt as if I had just missed a game-winning play. After my pitiful rant retelling the story, she asked me what I was going to do next.

"I messed up, Dr. Hudson. I'm just gonna go to my room and try to do better in rehearsal tonight."

"So you're gonna let this little mishap allow you to miss out on this once-in-a-lifetime moment?"

"Yeah," I replied.

"No you're not, you're not a quitter. Put your smile back on and at least enjoy the show."

Dr. Hudson knew that the Ray Charles postage stamp event was bigger than my shame. She knew that I would at least enjoy the concert and enjoy being part of that historic moment.

After our conversation, I felt better. I knew that this mistake was indeed a failure, but not fatal. I walked back over to the Ray Charles Performing Arts Center and sat in the back. It was crazy because as soon as I sat in my seat, an announcer came on the loudspeaker and said, "Ladies and gentlemen, please welcome R&B sensation Ashanti."

The auditorium erupted into thunderous applause and there she was, Ashanti on stage singing her classic hits. I was floored. I had never seen a celebrity so close before. I had no idea that Ashanti would be there.

She was up there doing her thing. During Ashanti's performance I thought how cool it would be to get a picture with her. The day had already been long and hard, but I wanted it all to mean something. Once Ashanti left the stage I ran around the building looking for the superstar I had been listening to for years.

I went around the entire perimeter of the building. I went to every exit and door. I found myself in the back of the Ray Charles Performing Arts Center in a small parking lot that had a black Suburban in it. My curiosity subsided when I saw a campus police officer standing near the Suburban. This officer had to be the man who would tell me what I needed to know.

"Excuse me, sir. Do you know where Ashanti will be?"

"Yes sir, are you a freshman this year?"

The officer was amiable. I'm sure he knew that I was a freshman because of my ambition and zeal, and we hit it off instantly. I told the officer about the rough day I had. He said he would help me out as long as I followed his instruction.

"When she comes out just relax, and I promise you, you'll get your picture."

Time went by; I started to get discouraged and sad again. After about fifteen minutes of dry silence and being on my phone, I heard some heels clicking down the hallway.

"Here she comes," said the officer. "Stay alert."

I looked up to my right and there was Ashanti and her entourage walking toward the officer and me. As she reached the building's exit the officer said to her, "Excuse me, Ashanti, this young man wants to get a picture with you."

Once Ashanti set foot outside of the building I got a full view of what she looked like. She was stunning. She wore a long, fitted, white dress and had on the best perfume.

"Is your camera ready? We're a little behind, but if you're ready, I am."

Ashanti's speaking voice was so sweet. After she spoke, I quickly tossed my iPhone to the officer so he could take my picture with Ashanti.

We posed for the picture, and there it was. I got my picture with Ashanti! My day had completely turned around. I walked back to my dorm satisfied that I didn't let the actions of the morning deter the entire day.

Following the conversation I had with Dr. Hudson I went back to the auditorium and tried again. I tried to make the best of the situation. I tried to make the day worth more than my disappointment. I tried, and it worked. The picture I took with Ashanti is one of my all-time favorites and it made Dr. Hudson so happy when she saw it. You should have seen the look on her face when I told her how I turned the situation around by making the choice to not give up.

The story perfectly embodies what can happen when you don't let the events of a single moment ruin your entire day. Always keep going. There will be times when you go to do something and it won't go as planned.

I woke up later than I thought I should. I got dressed in the outfit that I thought was right and it was still wrong. I failed myself, and I failed the glee club. As I walked out of the auditorium, I was so disappointed in myself that I almost let that moment ruin my entire day. If I would have given up and gone to my room, I would have never met Ashanti. I wouldn't have this melodramatic story to tell you about how I tried again.

Keep going no matter what. Keep a positive attitude even when things don't go your way. Like the popular Ashanti song "Dreams" says, "Dreams are real, all you have to do is just believe." Belief helps to manifest our dreams and desires. In order to manifest any dream it is important to keep trying even if things don't work out. Trying again enhances your chances for success, even if it's just by one percent. Always remember: Try again.

WAYS TO DEAL

When the Failure Initially Happens

- Accept how you feel
  - Of course it will hurt when you've just failed. Accept the moment for what it is and accept how you feel.
  - After you have truly accepted it, move on. Don't dwell in that negative thinking.
  - What happened in the past didn't happen in the past, it happened in the present. Whatever will happen in the future hasn't happened yet, so either way stay present. Once the situation has passed, release it and let it go.

- Separate yourself from the situation
  - You are not your failures. When I failed tests I used to say, "I am a bad math student" instead of, "I did poorly on one test." There's a difference in those two statements. One is defining me, the person, while the other defines a situation. Aim to label your situations; don't label yourself.

- Look for areas where you can learn
  - Socrates once stated, "The unexamined life is not worth living." In any situation with failure look for

areas you can improve so you don't repeat the same action again.

Looking at failures as a means to grow, rather than a situation that has failed you, will help you improve in life. Take responsibility.

4

FRESHMAN FINANCES

"A fool and his money are soon parted."

—American proverb

The freshman fifteen is an alliteration that worries many young college students. Everyone warned me about the freshman fifteen in school, and boy do I wish I had been listening. One alliteration that I wasn't lucky enough to be warned about was freshman finances. I wish I had prepared for college finances. In high school I held down part-time jobs in retail and fast food. When I went to college no one ever told me that life as I knew it would change forever. There would be nights when I had to eat ramen noodles and turn down chances to go out with friends because I couldn't afford it, and each semester I would have to find ways to purchase textbooks.

The reality of dealing with college is that to minimize stress, it's imperative to deal with finances actively. Looking back on my time at Morehouse there were so many financial decisions that I wish I would have made differently. To this day I'm still paying for some of the poor financial decisions I made in college. I hope that after hearing about my blunders of financial disaster you make better decisions than I did while in undergrad.

Food & Dining

In high school I hated the cafeteria food. It was like the stereotypical high school cafeteria food you see on TV. There were Mystery Meat Mondays, Trash Thursdays—it was terrible. I think because I went to a HBCU the food options were slightly better. One of my favorite days of the week was Wednesday, Fried Chicken Wednesday. The cafeteria was a way to connect with my classmates and enjoy a meal that I would not have to cook.

Cooking wasn't an option for me because I stayed in a dorm-style living space. Some students lived in the suites, which came with a full-functioning kitchen. Unfortunately, I was not one of those lucky students, so my meals came from the cafe. My advice to anyone who plans to live on-campus during his or her time in undergrad is to secure a meal plan that will allow you to utilize your cafeteria. Meal plans are usually paid for through your cost of attendance (your total cost for school including tuition, room and board), and will save you the trips you'll take if you always eat out.

One time I wanted to flex and feel cool, so I invited my best friend Sean to go out to eat with me. Sean is the ying to my yang.

Together we always have crazy adventures and make great memories. When I want to hang with someone and do something daring, I can always count on Sean to be down for the ride. This instance was no different.

It was Tuesday so I knew we should hit a Mexican spot in Midtown Atlanta for some tacos to celebrate Taco Tuesday. Of course Sean agreed and we decided to go to Prickly Pear Taqueria. Prickly Pear was a hit amongst us students in the AUC. The bartenders made great pitchers, they served incredible tacos, and the food was filling. Sean and I knew that we were going to have a great time and eat lots of tacos. Neither of us had cars at the time, so we decided to take an Uber from campus.

I ordered the Uber from my phone, and we headed to the front of campus to get picked up by our driver. As we walked to the car, we noticed someone in the passenger seat. We both knew this was weird, but we didn't care. We didn't want to wait for another Uber, so we decided to get in the car and head to Taco Tuesday at Prickly Pear.

While we were in the car there was a moment of awkward silence. Sean looked at me, I looked at him. Neither of us knew how to feel about the passenger in the Uber. About a mile into the trip, the Uber driver finally spoke.

"So y'all go to Morehouse?" the driver asked.

"Yeah, we're students. I'm from Ohio and Sean is from Minnesota," I replied.

"Oh that's cool. What are y'all about to get into?"

Sean spoke. "We're headed to Midtown to get some tacos and be lit."

"Oh really? I love tacos. Me and my friend just had some the other day."

In the back seat with my credit card and my limit I knew that I could confidently invite this Uber driver and her passenger to join us for food.

"Well, why don't you join us? Sean and I are cool. Let's all get some food together, my treat."

Sean nudged me discreetly after I extended the invitation. I'm sure he knew that I didn't have the money to be out splurging on an Uber driver and her friend whom we had just met. But it was too late. I already asked the question. I thought maybe the Uber driver would be busy and turn us down, until she said, "All right cool. Let's all go."

We all headed to Prickly Pear for Taco Tuesday.

When we arrived, it was the perfect setup. There were just enough people at the restaurant—it wasn't boring, but it wasn't too crowded. When the waiter began taking our orders we each ordered lots of food. We ordered wings, margaritas, and most importantly, tacos. It was a fun time. Everyone was smiling, enjoying the food and drinks, until the bill came. When the waiter passed me the bill, I grabbed it.

The bill read $123.19. As I looked at the bill, all I could do was gasp. The tab was the equivalent of one of my cell phone bills. By this time what choice did I have? I had already told everyone that I was going to pay, and we had such a good time. After eating my last taco, I slid my card into the bill envelope slot and paid the $123.19 for some tacos and drinks.

That was by far one of the biggest financial mistakes that I made while in school. My mindset was not about saving and being financially secure while in college; I simply spent the money because I knew that I wanted to look cool and eat some tacos.

I tell you this story so you don't make the same mistake I did. I should have gone to the cafeteria that night and played it easy, but I didn't. Food and drinks are an expensive luxury that you may have to sacrifice while in college. Try to refrain from impulsive decisions like the ones I made in my Prickly Pear incident. Of course, that was a nice dinner and it taught me a valuable lesson, but I'm sure that Uber driver and her friend don't even remember my name.

If it isn't a friend's birthday or a very special occasion, eat on campus and save your money. Don't go to Prickly Pear and blow $130, doing so will just make you feel like an idiot days after.

I learned a lot from this experience. This valuable experience taught me about saving and not compulsively spending to look cool.

Saving

Preparation is one way to avoid financial disasters. When I got to Morehouse, I had forty dollars in my pocket and no money in the bank. I had blown all of my earnings for college on things that I thought I would need down in Atlanta, like an iPhone with an everything plan.

As you prepare to make your way into college, prepare early and do so wisely. If you're working part-time and making some money, do your best to save money and put some aside for college. Banks will happily help you set up a savings account that you can only use in case of real emergencies. In high school, I was all about making money and blowing it entirely on All-Star Chuck Taylors and T-shirts from Hot Topic. It would have served me a lot better to save some of that money I was making and invest it in a proper savings account for when I went off to college.

College Discounts

There are so many companies and restaurants that give student discounts. There's no need to spend necessary funds paying full price if you can get a discount. I always make it a point to inquire about student discounts and keep my college ID on me at all times.

Textbooks

I read online that the average student spends $1,000 a year on textbooks alone. I didn't quite reach $1,000, but I did get close my first semester of college. I bought every single textbook on all of my syllabi. I came to learn that not every book is necessary simply because it appears on a syllabus.

There may be instances when a professor creates a list of books that she will "require" each student to purchase. This list may not always be permanent. I had a course where we did not get to all of the readings in the class. There were courses where classes would get caught up in discussions; we would have weather delays that put us out of classes; and we simply wouldn't get to the end of the syllabus. Make it a point to buy textbooks as you need them during your semester. I understand that you may want to be prepared, as I did, but sometimes over preparing with your books can cause you to overspend.

Textbooks can also be found for better prices online. Chegg. com and Amazon.com are two of many websites on which you can buy your textbooks. Amazon has Amazon Prime, which enables more items to be delivered next-day (if available). Do your best to find these deals and spend less on your textbooks.

Upperclassmen can also be a resource for textbooks. Everyone in the same major takes similar academic paths. Your fellow upperclassmen may have taken the same class that you are taking now, maybe even with the same professor.

Early in my Morehouse tenure I was enrolled in a business law class. There was a business law book that was listed in the bookstore at Morehouse for $349. I had no idea what I was going to do. I noticed that one of my brothers who was in the glee club with me was in the course. He had an e-book version that he emailed to me so I could have the textbook for that class.

E-books are another more affordable alternative to getting the textbooks you desire. Ask your professor if e-books are available for the textbook you are looking to buy.

Budgeting

When you know that you have lots of things to buy, budgeting is one way to track where all your money is going. Whether you are going to create a spreadsheet, use a notebook or mobile app, you should have some conscious way to determine what money is coming in and what is going out. The important part is to find a budgeting system that works for you.

Some common ways to begin budgeting:

- Understand your net income
- How much money is coming in?
- Track your spending
  - Make a note of every dollar you spend.

- Set realistic goals for the things you want to buy
  - Your financial goals don't have to be permanent, but by understanding what you want, you can plan for it better.

- Implement a plan
  - After you know how much money you earn and how much you spend, you can determine how much you can save.
  - Once you find income, you can determine how much you need to save to accomplish your goals.
- Stick to the budget
  - Budgeting only works if you work it over time.
  - Stay disciplined and be hard on yourself—the rewards are plentiful.

During my time in undergrad I used the Bank of America My-Portfolio tool. The MyPortfolio from Bank of America consists of a financial dashboard filled with a helpful variety of tools to help individuals manage money. You'll need a savings or checking account to sign up for the service, but if you have another account at another bank, the MyPortfolio app allows you to sync your account with the service by entering your online login information. The tool helps track how much money is being deposited into your account, what your expenses are, and where you are spending the most money. Visually, the app is very appealing as it provides bar graphs that categorize your spending. There are other budgeting services offered by banks such as Citi Financial tools, Wells Fargo My Money Map and more. Ask your bank what budgeting services they offer and start tracking your savings while in college.

Credit Cards

In college no one has money. Most college students are struggling and looking for a way to make some passive income. Instead of working for money, I've witnessed peers sign up for credit cards so they can still spend freely although they don't have a job. Credit cards are very easy to get in college. If you have some work history and have never signed up for a credit card, companies will be begging you to sign up. Whatever you do, proceed with caution. I'm not preaching that you totally abandon the idea of getting a credit card, but if you do decide to proceed, be mindful of a credit card's life-altering effects.

A lot of credit card companies have high interest rates. This "rate" means that if you get a credit card and you purchase a pair of sunglasses for only fifty dollars, you may end up paying sixty-five dollars for the same sunglasses if you let that purchase earn interest. This standard interest rate is called an annual percentage rate, often abbreviated as APR. When reviewing the terms and conditions of a credit card you may find that there are a number of different APRs. Each applies to different costs from your financial organization. There is a penalty APR, which is a rate you will be charged if you don't pay the minimum amount of credit card payments due within sixty days. Balance transfer APR; if you transfer an old balance onto your new credit card, it will accrue interest at this rate. The most commonly understood rate is the purchase APR; this rate is the one applied to all purchases you make with your credit card. This type of APR is the only interest rate commonly discussed, and will be addressed in this chapter.

The purchase APR on a credit card can vary depending on the person and the credit card. At the time of this book's publication, Discover offered a credit card with a 0% introductory APR on purchases and balance transfers for fourteen months. After the introductory APR period ended, the purchase APR would be 11.74% and the balance transfer APR would be 23.74%. Citibank offered a longer introductory APR period—twenty-one months—after which period the purchase APR increased to 14.49% and the balance transfer rate to 24.49%.

APR rates vary depending on your creditworthiness. Always make it a point to inquire about APRs when you are applying for a credit card. As our economy grows and changes, so will credit cards and annual percentage rates. Monitor the APRs on your credit cards and pay your balances if you manage to get one.

Most credit cards offer a grace period of at least twenty-one days. This period is from the time of purchase to the time that your credit card payment is due. Most banks accumulate interest daily, using a method called average daily balance. If you can find a way to pay off your balance in full within the grace period, you will get to skip paying interest on that balance. Do your best to only buy items that you can pay for in full, with cash, within the next twenty-one days. If you can't purchase an item with cash within twenty-one days, then don't buy it with a credit card. Spending within your means allows you to control your interest rates, saving you money.

I got myself a student credit card during my time in undergrad. I had a $900 limit on my credit card and just went crazy. I was at brunches; I was getting haircuts and doing all kinds of things that I did not need to do, just to keep up with my friends. The worst part was when those credit card bills came in, and I was unable to pay them. By continually defaulting on my credit card payments my credit score was severely affected.

A credit score is what lenders, banks, and many other financial institutions use to determine whether they should lend you credit or not. The higher your credit score, the better your chances of securing credit and economic mobility. Credit scores range from 300–850. A credit score over 700 is considered to be good. A score of 800 or more on the same scale is deemed to be excellent. According to Experian.com, most credit scores are between 600–750; this is average. There are many different kinds of companies that can provide you with a credit rating, but the two most common are the FICO score and the VantageScore.

Think of your credit score like a report card at the end of the semester. Just like a report card is a general indicator of where you are academically, your credit score assesses where you are financially. When you attempt to buy a house, your credit score will be a major indicator in determining whether or not you are financially responsible enough to do so. There are also other times when your credit scores may be considered, like when you're applying for a loan or leasing a cell phone.

Before considering any major financial decisions such as signing up for a credit card, seek professional help. As you transition into college, make it a priority to get your credit score and monitor it carefully. If you decide to sign up for a credit card, understand that it may affect your score and could have severe life consequences. I have talked to so many people whose credit scores got messed up in college because they signed up for credit cards. Don't be one of those people. Be careful. The last thing you need on top of exams, peer pressure, and the stress of classes is credit card stress.

Relationships and Food

When you get tired of the cafeteria food and do want to cook, make a point to do so collaboratively. You can have a group of friends pitch in on groceries, and you all cook together and split the cost. This collaborative effort to cook food will not only help you sharpen your cooking and grocery shopping skills, but will also help you form great relationships.

Relationships and getting involved on campus will also save you money. One way to get different kinds of foods on campus is by attending all the school events that provide free food. During my time in college I would go to every event I could if they had free food, and most events usually did. Social groups are always advertising events on campus; take advantage of all the free food you can get.

Employment

Later in this book I'll give you tips to help you secure a job. There is nothing wrong with working on campus to make some extra money. There are lots of money-making opportunities right on your campus. Seek them and be open to the idea of working part-time. If you're a great writer, some students may even pay you to assist them with writer's block or crafting essays. If you find that you are a star math student, you could charge your peers for math tutoring. Although a structured part-time job may be overwhelming, see if you can offer a professional service to your peers for some passive income.

Every little bit counts. After my undergraduate experience, I can say for sure that there will be times when money is short, but you never want to make the situation harder on yourself than it has to be. Dealing with college is tough as is, so make it a priority to make smart financial decisions that will lead you toward a time in undergrad when you're financially free.

WARNING: Before making any major financial decision during your time in college, consult with a financial expert. All of the aforementioned advice stems from things I learned through mere Google searches, conversations with bankers, and my own experiences. This chapter by no means should be the end of your personal finance education. Keep learning.

WAYS TO DEAL

When You Consider Getting a Credit Card

- Seriously consider the impact a credit card could have on your finances

When You Are Making Money Before Going to College

- Save your money

When You Are in College

- Save your money

When You Are Asked to Do Anything

- Save your money

⑤

INVEST IN YOU

"The best investment you can make is in yourself."

—Warren Buffett

I've become quite the reader. I love reading. During my time in undergrad, I would often sit in my room with a book in hand and read. I think we should make as much of an effort to exercise our minds with fervent reading, as we invest in exercising our bodies with physical activities. I didn't become a reader until my sophomore year of college. It all started when I learned that one of my favorite speakers in the world was coming to town.

It was an evening like any other. By this time I was a sophomore, more confident this semester than the last. I was headed to my dorm after classes and started to do my routine check of social media. I scrolled through Facebook and read the usual incessant posts detailing complaints, child updates, and aspirations written by all my Facebook friends. As I was on the Facebook app, I got a notification from Twitter that said Oprah had tweeted.

Oprah has always been one of my favorite public figures and inspirations. All of her tweets are sent to my phone so I can keep up with what she says. This particular tweet announced that Oprah would be going on #TheLifeYouWantTour. This tour included a list of cities that Oprah and other spiritual leaders would visit offering lectures, workshops, and advice to all who attended. Of the cities on the list that Oprah and her team would visit, Atlanta was at the very top. I was so ecstatic. I thought this was my chance to finally see Oprah live in action, and witness her doing what she does best.

I quickly did some research to see where the event would take place and how much tickets would cost. The tickets were around $700. I had just arrived back to school; I had no idea where I was going to get the money to attend the Oprah ATL weekend seminar. I asked everyone I knew at Morehouse if they had any ties to Oprah or access to tickets. I was ambitious and hopeful. I even emailed my school president at the time. Sadly, everywhere I looked I was turned down.

A few days later, I got another notification that Oprah was releasing a book titled *What I Know For Sure*. I told myself that if I couldn't go to the seminar, the least I could do was buy and read the book. That afternoon I went to the campus bookstore, and to my surprise the book was at the register, on display, and for sale. I had not anticipated purchasing the book that day; I thought I would have to request it and wait a couple of days before I got it. To my surprise, the book was right there in my face as I went to leave the bookstore. I knew that this was a divine moment because at the same time I wanted that particular book, it just happened to be in the bookstore. I quickly bought the book, returned to my room and got to reading.

What I Know For Sure was a phenomenal book, and with the turn of every page I felt as if I was having a conversation with Oprah. I sat there and read ten pages, which turned into chapters, and before I knew it, I had finished the entire book in one sit down. That was the first time I had read an entire book in a long time. I couldn't believe I enjoyed reading that much, but I did. The book left me feeling inspired, hopeful and happy.

The next day I knew that I couldn't give up on my journey to attend Oprah's seminar in Atlanta. *What I Know For Sure* discussed themes of optimism, overcoming fear and living your best life. The book inspired me to get creative and get focused. I knew that I wanted to go to the Life You Want Tour, and I knew that if I could just focus enough I could come up with a way to make it happen. I had one last trick up my sleeve; my goal was to email an employee from Harpo, the company that Oprah had founded. I met this woman via Twitter. Her name was Maya. (Crazy, right? Another Maya.) She and I had a good relationship on Twitter, and I always thought she was very kind.

After an email dialogue, she quickly said she could help. She sent me a PDF of a ticket, and it was up from there. The event was that weekend, and all I could do was smile. As life would have it, I went to the seminar and had a blast. The Oprah's Life You Want Weekend was phenomenal. I went with my best friend Ryan George, and we had a fun time. Ryan and I were amazed by how excited everyone was. We had never seen so many people getting along so well and so happy. Ryan and I laughed and enjoyed ourselves. Before I knew it, the lights went dim, and a video came on the screen. It was Oprah. I recognized her voice instantly.

The video was a trailer highlighting some of Oprah's biggest moments. After the conclusion of the trailer, Oprah rose out of the stage on a platform, made her way down some stairs and hit center stage. She looked stunning in a beautiful red gown. Her hair flowed in the wind as she walked to the center stage. It was like a scene out of a movie. I couldn't help but cheer.

Oprah gave an impressive, emotional speech about all the things she went through. The speech and lessons that I learned from that lecture resonated with me deeply. It was like reading the book but even better because there was Oprah, actually in front of me, in the building, breathing the same air as I was. It was a moment I will never forget.

After Ryan and I left that seminar we reflected on the lecture on the car ride back to campus. Ryan was hilarious and kept making jokes about everything we had seen. As we talked about the seminar, I tweeted about how exciting the event was.

I tweeted: "@LifeYouWantTour I almost started shouting when she said 'Nothing we've gone thru will be wasted,' my God that was good #LifeYouWantATL"

The Oprah Winfrey Life You Want weekend was a two-day event. The Oprah lecture on Friday was just part one; the classroom and interactive piece were on Saturday. The morning of Saturday came and I was ready for part two. Ryan was busy that weekend, and I was kind of bummed because I knew that I would have to go by myself. When I made it to the Phillips Arena, I got settled and was ready to have a good time. There was a DJ in the house and everyone was enjoying what had become a dance party in the arena.

As the music kicked up a notch, Oprah again made her way to center stage. Everyone went nuts yet again. Oprah began this session reflecting on the dynamic night we had the night before.

"I read some of your tweets last night from the event," Oprah said.

I sat there listening as I knew I was part of the tweetfest from last night.

"Here are some of the tweets I saw."

I looked to the left where the titantron was placed. As I looked up I saw my tweet on the screen.

Oprah said, "Chris Sumlin tweeted last night, 'I almost started shouting when she said "Nothing we've gone thru will be wasted," my God that was good.'"

I instantly jumped out of my seat screaming, "Oprah that's me! Oprah! Oprah!"

Oprah didn't hear me, but just hearing the name "Chris Sumlin" roll off her tongue, and knowing that she was talking about me, was a feeling I can't describe. All I remember is that my hands were sweaty, my heart felt like it was going to explode out of my chest, and I felt more alive than ever.

It should go without saying that you should never give up on your goals. Whenever you have a dream that may seem out of reach, use this story as a reminder of how important it is to never give up. Sometimes our goals are big, and we have no idea how we can accomplish them. When I decided I wanted to see Oprah I didn't know who to ask, how it would happen or what I would do, but I never gave up.

The weekend I got to see Oprah in Atlanta was one of the highlights of my fall—an experience I easily could have missed had I not been persistent and sent that last email. In college there are so many goals you may have that seem inconceivable, but the important part is to never give up. You have to keep the vision and believe a way will be made.

I deeply enjoyed learning outside of the classroom. This entire journey of getting to the seminar made me realize the importance and joy of reading. The encouragement I received from Oprah's book *What I Know For Sure* kept me going. It allowed me to press on even when I thought I wouldn't find a way. After I finished that book, I kept reading. I wanted to dip inside the minds of other people I admired through their writings and books. After the Oprah seminar weekend I wanted to go to more conferences where I could get insightful knowledge. I think this desire to reach further outside of my academic coursework has placed me lightyears ahead of my peers.

I invest time to make sure that I work on passion projects. I invest time into reading intellectually stimulating books to keep myself sharp on a variety of topics. Billionaire investor Chris Sacca was speaking to a crowd once when he said the one thing he looks for when hiring potential employees is an ability to speak on a multitude of topics.

"Those kinds of people are just more interesting," Sacca said.

College is great, but it can be very linear. The actual coursework by itself doesn't teach essential skills to help us deal with this thing called life. From my experience, I can say that the books I've read, TED Talks I've watched, and conferences I've attended on top of my formal education have helped me tremendously.

Do your schoolwork, put forth your best effort, and excel in your academics. Conversely, don't be afraid to read a book for fun or attend a conference. Dr. Martin Luther King once stated, "Intelligence plus character is the goal of education." I can say with confidence that investing in your mind outside of your academics is a good way to achieve that purpose.

WAYS TO DEAL

When You Have a Book You Want to Read

- Consult with the bookstore manager at your school to see if he or she can have the book delivered to your campus store
- Buy audiobooks to help you read faster
  - You'll be surprised how quickly our brains can hear and process information. Buying audiobooks and increasing the speed will allow you to read books a lot faster.
- Read when you have less going on
  - Early morning is my favorite time to read because I know that I have a lesser chance of being distracted.
  - Academics are a priority, but there are always weekends and semester breaks, which make for terrific times to read.

When You Want to Learn Something New Outside of School

- Use your smartphone to learn

- There are so many informative videos on YouTube that can aid you in learning about an array of different topics.

- Subscribe to news publications
  - Popular news publications like the *New York Times* offer student discounts that allow you to access their entire daily newspaper through your smartphone or mobile device. Reading publications like the *New York Times* is a great way to stay hip to all that is going on in the world.

When a Conference Comes to Town

- Plan ahead to attend conferences so you can prepare properly
  - Most major conferences are announced a year in advance to allow time for interested audiences to prepare to attend. Make it a habit to search for conferences that are coming to your area while in school.

- Ask for student discounts
  - Many conferences will provide students with discount codes that allow them to attend conferences at a discounted rate. Look for these opportunities when looking to attend a conference.

- Ask to volunteer
  - Every conference and event needs workers to make sure it is run smoothly and properly. Ask around to see if anyone will let you volunteer to attend a conference or engagement.

6

FEELING FOR THE FIT

"Your intuition is the most honest friend that you will ever have."
—Doe Zantamata

"Man up, get out of your feelings" is a statement I hear far too often. There seems to be this constant message encouraging people to numb how they feel about things. With the rapid decline of engaging face-to-face interactions due to technology, we are rarely fully in tune with others, and more importantly, less in tune with ourselves.

This self-induced emotional numbing is a dangerous phenomenon that is taking over our society. Of course, I love social media, texting, and interacting with my friends online, who doesn't? But the memories I value more than our text conversations are the ones created when we are having so much fun we forget to take pictures. The memories made when I'm fully present and unplugged.

I've also come to enjoy these moments when I'm by myself.

Every day I allow myself thirty minutes, during which time I unplug, reflect, and evaluate what's going on in my life. These instances allow me to silence the noise of everything that's going on around me and get still. In these moments of stillness, I can feel and be free in my skin. This practice has allowed me to make decisions that are more intentional and focused on me.

During midterms in my sophomore year of college I had to make a decision for myself that would be one of my biggest and most personal yet.

Coming into Morehouse, I never did heavy research on what I wanted to study. I knew I enjoyed computers, so I thought maybe I'd major in computer science and work for a tech company. My mother always told me I'd make a great lawyer, so I considered majoring in political science to prepare myself for law school. As my time in high school came to an end, I decided that I was going to major in business administration with a concentration in marketing. During the summer before Morehouse, I had done some consulting work with a small candle selling business. The work was easy and stimulating, so I assumed I'd go to college to learn marketing and start my own consulting firm following my undergrad experience. That was my plan.

When I was graduating from high school I told everyone who would listen that I was going to college to pursue a business degree. As I expressed how I wanted to help small minority-owned businesses, the individuals I talked to were so impressed. I would hear statements such as:

"That's a good career choice; business majors make all the money."

"You'll never be without work with that degree."

And most importantly:

"That's a degree that will help with that student loan debt."

With the validation I received from everyone else, I assumed I was making a great decision. I knew for sure that this sense of security did not come from me. I never deeply reflected on what I wanted to do in the world or who I wanted to be. I simply rambled off some dream that I knew would impress others, because I wanted the people to whom I was talking to be impressed. This big decision—what I would study, what I would do with my life—was all rooted in a quick sense of validation from others.

Once the time came for me to start taking my business classes, everything I assumed about my major and career path was put to the test. I took classes such as business law and microeconomics early on. One of my favorite classes was the business law course I took. My professor, Vince Eagan, was one of my favorite professors during my time at Morehouse. He was a fair-skinned, thin man with glasses. He always wore a suit, began class with jokes about football, and encouraged dialogue in class. Professor Eagan was fantastic, but my peers in the class weren't. The brothers in my classes wore suits and ties. They enjoyed discussing concepts like stocks, assets, and other business-related topics that I didn't find interesting. I felt very out of my element in class.

Following this semester and my first taste of business classes, I persevered. This time I took Accounting I. This course was taught by Professor Hollis. Again, a great professor and person, but I dreaded going to class. The concepts we learned in accounting went right over my head. In week one, we learned about debits and credits. Once week two came around and we started talking about depreciation, I was so lost.

My sense of ignorance was tested when it came time to take our first accounting exam. The test was four hours long and took place in the evening. I'll never forget taking that exam. Fifteen minutes in I was completely overwhelmed with anxiety.

I considered myself to be a decent student. I understood that not every class would be a slice of cake. But this class felt different. After about an hour of filling in what I recollected from class and doing my best, I stopped taking my test. I couldn't even focus on the exam. In that moment, I started thinking about why I was taking this class and what it meant for my future. I reflected on my discomfort in my previous business classes. It was at this moment that I knew I was not going to move forward as a business major.

As the exam was in session, I decided I would wait until the first person was done with his exam and follow right behind him shortly after. About two hours into the exam I saw one of my classmates stand and turn in his exam. This was the moment I had been waiting for, but I wasn't sure if I should just hop up directly after. I began rocking back and forth in my seat. I turned and looked at everyone else. All of my peers had their heads in their test booklets, looking visibly focused. I didn't want to compare myself to the other guys in the room because I knew what mattered was me and how I felt. I dropped my pencil and made the decision that I was going to leave. As I had already decided what I was going to do, I instantly got up behind that guy and turned in my exam. The brother who turned in his exam before me probably did so because he actually aced the exam. I, on the other hand, knew I had failed and was just looking to leave the class as soon as possible. With my decision made, I turned in my exam and I walked out feeling relieved.

I don't know why, but after I was out of the doorway I started running. If you've ever seen the scene in the film *Precious* where the main character runs out of the chicken restaurant, imagine me doing that same exact kind of running. I had no idea where I was running, but I knew I was running the heck out of the Walter E. Massey Leadership Center where business classes were held. I knew inside myself that this would be the last accounting exam I would take, and that I was going to find a major that felt right.

During my semester with Accounting I, I had space for an

elective on my schedule. With this space I took a course called Introduction to Television. The course was offered under the Cinema, Television and Emerging Media Studies (CTEMS) program. I loved the class. It was three hours long, but it felt like ten minutes. Professor Adisa Iwa taught the class. Professor Iwa was the man. Each class consisted of relevant topics and stimulating discussions that taught us the art of creating television.

During midterm week I had a midterm in Introduction to Television just like I had previously in Accounting I. The test wasn't four hours, but it was three. The midterm for this course was long and required a level of competence that took studying. As I took this exam I felt very different from when I had taken my Accounting I exam. I really enjoyed Intro to TV and the course concepts came to me easily. In this class, I always participated, the lectures were fun, and everything felt familiar. The exam was even fun. Luckily, since it was material that I was familiar with, I was confident and took the test quickly. Recalling the information came easily. It was a far better experience than my time with the accounting exam.

Just like in my Accounting I exam, I knew I wanted to finish relatively quickly to get out of the class. I vividly remember finishing this exam first, but it wasn't because I guessed or was trying to leave. I finished first because I knew the material. I walked out of that exam feeling confident that I did my best and predicting that my grade would reflect my efforts.

My midterm grades for that semester were what I anticipated. I earned a "D" for my performance in my Accounting I class and an "A+" in my Introduction to Television course. These midterm grades were the final straw for me. I knew that the business department was not serving me in the way that I desired. I wanted to feel alive when I was in class and deeply engaged. I didn't want to sit in a class simply because it was the major that everyone else thought I should take. I wanted to be happy and rooted in what I wanted to study. Following that midterm week, I dropped my Accounting I class and I changed my major from business administration to cinema, television and emerging media studies. That next semester I started making better grades, and my classes were stimulating. My CTEMS classes were not drastically easier than the coursework of my business courses, but I enjoyed the process of learning from these courses, and it felt right. Once I got in my major, I felt that it was where I belonged.

The lesson I took away from this was to get in my feelings and allow myself to follow my heart. I must say, in college, there are so many decisions you are going to make. Decisions about who your friends are, what you'll major in and what you spend your time doing. I invite you to get in your feelings. When we face a crossroads or have to decide between two difficult decisions, the answers that tell us what we need to do are never too far from our reach. The most important aspect of weighing a decision is truly assessing how you are feeling about the decision.

In college, there is a lot of peer pressure that may attempt to direct you in what you should be doing at all times. There will be moments when you will feel that you need to study, but you may have a friend who wants you to go out and party. There will be times when you feel you have a burning question in class, but you may talk yourself out of putting yourself forward and asking. These are perfect examples of when it is important to feel for the right fit and make a sound decision. In any given situation it is imperative that no matter what happens, you feel that you are making the best choices for yourself.

Your college experience is also one that is expensive. Tuition is continually getting more expensive. The financial investment you make by going to college is compelling enough to remind you to live your college experience for you.

Anyone who knows me knows that one of my all-time favorite singers is Beyoncé. I think that Beyoncé is easily the greatest performer of our generation. When I have free time, I love watching her behind-the-scenes videos where she explains her creative process. One night I was watching a Beyoncé video titled "What Happens in Vegas." The video gave an in-depth look into Beyoncé creating her Las Vegas show, I AM YOURS. There was a moment in the video where she was frustrated with her team about the stage setup for the show.

"It just doesn't feel right," she lamented.

In her mind, she had the vision of what her show was supposed to be, and she knew that what was transpiring was not in alignment with her vision. Beyoncé had the vision, got in her feelings and made the change when her feelings led her differently. Inevitably, the team took Beyoncé's instruction, and the show was fantastic. I'm sure it took great courage to tell everyone that a significant change needed to be made, but she persevered. How unfair would it have been to be considerate to all the members of her team and not herself?

Ultimately, it was her show and her name on the ticket that people purchased.

When a tough decision needs to be made it's important that we understand it is ultimately up to us to make the life we desire a reality. I knew that some people would not agree with my decision to change my major from business to CTEMS, but at the end of the day, I knew I was the one who would have to take those classes day in and day out. I had to do what felt right for me.

As you grow and start feeling for the right fit, you'll get better at it. Following your heart is a practice that takes time to develop. After you make this idea part of your practice, it becomes second nature. This lesson isn't to say you should be overly emotional and guided solely by your feelings. There are times when feelings can fool. Your core feelings in your heart are a good foundation to make a sound decision. I have a quote printed in my room that says,

"Follow your heart but don't forget to take your brain with you." This idea is important to remember. With an open mind and open heart, consider the risks and use reason, but never numb yourself so much that you can't feel your way to the right fit. You deserve it.

WAYS TO DEAL

When Choosing a Major

- Assess your talents
    - Look at the things you are naturally good at, the things on which you are often complimented. Maybe you are good with kids. If so, you may consider majoring in early child education. Maybe you love writing poetry, so you decide to major in English.
    - Understanding what you are naturally good at is a great base for finding a major that will fit your needs.
- Assess your efforts
    - What are the things you are good at that no one has to instruct you to do? What are the activities you do in your free time? The answers to these questions require some self-assessment, but will assist you in making a good decision in regard to what kind of major you may want to pursue.
- Think long term

○ After you have chosen a major and graduated, it is expected that you will be able to find a job and career with what you have learned. Every major has job opportunities. When evaluating what major you want to pursue, think of a job that you can obtain after using the skills you learned in college.

When Considering Dropping a Course

- Consult with your academic advisor; never make the decision to drop a course without first seeking advice from an advisor
  ○ Dropping a course can hugely impact your academic track and cause you to graduate late.

- Get help as soon as you see that you are falling behind
  ○ By the second week of my Accounting I class I knew that I was struggling, but I never discussed my frustrations with a professor. If you find yourself struggling talk to a professor as soon as possible.

When Considering Changing Majors

- Make the decision to change no later than the first semester of your junior year
  ○ Majors are defined by a certain number of credit

hours. If you are a senior trying to change majors you would have to make up all of those hours, which inevitably could make you graduate late.

- Consider taking on a minor
  - ○ If it is too late to change majors and you hate your major classes, consider adding a minor that you know you will particularly enjoy.
  - ○ If a minor would add too many hours, be intentional about signing up for elective courses that will be fun and stimulating for you.

(7)

MENTORS MATTER

"The delicate balance of mentoring someone is not creating them in your own image, but giving them the opportunity to create themselves."

—Steven Spielberg

We all know that college is full of possibilities and wonder. There are times when you may wonder what to wear, what to pursue and what to avoid. One way to avoid the many pitfalls of college is to surround yourself with active mentors. Looking back on my time at Morehouse, I wish I would have understood early on the value mentoring can have on anyone's collegiate journey. During my sophomore year, I made it a priority to ensure that I had a group of people I admired surround me in every aspect of my life. Whether it was my academic work, or even social status, I made sure that I had a list of go-to advisors who would help me grow as a college student.

A mentor can come in different forms; there is no one method of creating effective mentorship. These consultants may be those you call for advice, someone you bounce ideas off, or even a person you admire from afar. Whichever way you slice it, mentors are important. Your mentor should have integrity, be accomplished in whatever it is you aspire to do, but most importantly he or she should be someone you trust. During my time at Morehouse I had two powerful mentors I went to for lots of advice: Dr. Elania Hudson and Professor Adisa Iwa.

I met Dr. Hudson on Facebook while I was still in high school. Dr. Hudson had a way of telling me exactly what I needed to hear whenever it was necessary. When I arrived at Morehouse and expressed interest in majoring in business, serendipitously Dr. Hudson became my academic advisor. I felt it was fate that she was assigned to me. As my academic advisor, it was mandatory that we meet and discuss what my class schedule would look like for the following semesters. Although scheduling and course placement were the intentions of our meetings, Dr. Hudson would advise me on so much more. Although there were times when I was annoyed with her advice, Dr. Hudson had a way of forcing me out of my comfort zone that I learned to appreciate as I matured.

Neale Donald Walsch once said, "Life begins at the end of your comfort zone." That is one true statement. When I started college, everything about the experience threw me out of my comfort zone.

It was a new city, new people, and most importantly, a new school. This discomfort that I felt made me want to quickly find people I could be comfortable around and do things that I would normally do at home. I knew that this thinking and practice was a cop-out, and that if I truly wanted to grow into a better person I would need to try new things. Dr. Hudson was a catalyst for stretching me out of my comfort zone and helping me meet new people.

The single most important characteristic of a mentor is someone who sees your potential and will not let you do anything until that potential has been tapped into. I can recount so many memories of Dr. Hudson seeing more in me than I saw in myself. In one instance there was a lunch meeting I had with her in the Papa John's on campus where we discussed my future goals. In the moment, I met her at Papa John's because I knew she would buy my pizza and we would laugh about things on campus. I had no interest in discussing anything serious; all I wanted was pizza and laughs. Pizza and laughs. As we sat down at the table we shared some small talk, I ordered a pepperoni pizza, and then she asked me a big question.

"Mr. Sumlin, who do you want to be in the world and what do you want to do? This is the time in your life when you can really try things and go for it."

As the words left her lips, I got nervous. I began feeling uncomfortable. There were some dreams that were looming in my head, but none I was ready to admit to myself, let alone share with anyone.

With a forced smile on my face I replied, "I'd love to be a talk show host and inspire my viewers."

Dr. Hudson was fun and I think she enjoyed my company, but one thing she didn't joke about was personal goals. I knew that once I shared this dream with her she was going to find a way for me to get started on it that very day.

"Well looks like you should start a YouTube channel and get to creating," she said.

"I don't know about that. I don't have a camera. Who would watch that? How would I do it?"

"You already have everything you need. Use your cell phone, set up a setting for the videos, and start creating. You have no excuse not to start this. Your journey starts today."

In that very meeting, she insisted that I start creating content online that would captivate people with my storytelling. It was Dr. Hudson who told me to take my writing seriously and practice making YouTube videos. If it weren't for her wisdom and guidance, I probably wouldn't have launched my YouTube channel, had the confidence to build my website, or even write this very book.

Mentors are excellent sources of support and will encourage you to get about the business of bringing your goals to life. Dr. Hudson had her own accomplishments and way of doing things that worked. After she became an expert in her field, she saw potential in me and didn't give up until I pushed toward my dream. Dr.

Hudson's mentorship was useful; it helped bring out excellence in me that I didn't even know existed. I never thought to do YouTube videos or take myself seriously as a public speaker. It was my mentor who saw this potential in me and forced me to see it in myself. That is what mentorship does to a person, when done correctly.

Mentors hold us accountable and encourage us to do things that we could never imagine were possible. Dr. Hudson's focus was in marketing while my focus was in inspirational storytelling. Because of her strong understanding of goal-setting and execution, she became an incredible mentor for me.

Another type of mentor is someone who has already been exactly where you want to go and can help you get there faster. Professor Adisa Iwa was a perfect mentor who did this for me.

I graduated from Morehouse with a degree in cinema, television and emerging media studies. The first course I ever took in that program was a class called Introduction to Television. Intro to TV was taught by a Morehouse alum named Professor Adisa Iwa. Professor Iwa will be remembered as one of my all-time favorite professors. When I first saw him I felt like we could even be related. We were both black, had the same skin tone, and similar views on life. He would always wear button-downs and jeans, just like I would. When he walked into a room he was filled with positive energy and was eager to teach us everything he knew. Every class he would say, "I want you guys to be super-duper mega successful so when I watch you on TV I can say, 'Hey that's my student.'" Early on I understood that Professor Iwa was not just interested in his own personal achievements, but in making sure that he equipped us with some incredible tools so we could make our own.

I enjoyed his class and sought out his advice regularly. There were times when I would come to class early just to have dialogue with Professor Iwa about the TV industry. Before I knew it, Professor Iwa and I had built a great relationship, and he became another one of my mentors. I admired his work in television and saw that he was a real-life example of what I could become if I worked hard enough. Professor Iwa also encouraged me verbally every class.

"Mr. Sumlin you're going to do great things."

"Mr. Sumlin you're smart and talented."

I'm not sure if teachers and professors realize the dynamic impact they make on students with their words. When Professor Iwa complimented me I felt good, and I believe I performed well in his class because his words gave me the foundation and confidence to take the coursework seriously. Although Professor Iwa was kind-hearted, he was big on telling it how it was and had no problem telling me when I was wrong.

I'll never forget the time at Morehouse when there was an industry panel on campus. In college there will be lots of recruiters on campus looking to find students to hire. Whenever you hear of these kinds of events and opportunities, go to them and at least see what you can learn. This industry panel at Morehouse was a chance for me to snag a potential summer job and I wanted to give it my best. By this time I had just changed my major to CTEMS and was moving toward the end of my sophomore year. Sophomore year is a terrific time to start applying for professional internships within your major. During this time in your collegiate career you should be finished with 80% if not all of your general education courses and be aware of your major. There are some exceptions to this rule, but it is generally understood that students begin their major coursework upon entering their junior year. I knew this principle and wanted to start my junior year with some internship experience. I understood that if I wanted an internship in my field, for the summer of my sophomore year, I had to do really well at this panel event.

Professor Iwa invited the entire class to attend the industry panel. He told us there would be food and that if we wanted to get an internship we should attend. Following that class session I approached Professor Iwa and we talked in his office.

As we entered Professor Iwa's office, I knew what my goal was, but I was not sure how I would achieve it. If there was anyone who could give me insight I knew Professor Iwa could. At any kind of career fair or panel, most everyone goes into the situation with the same goal: to get an internship or job. I understood that if everyone's goal was the same, my approach had to be different, flawless and unique.

When I sat with Professor Iwa, all my ambition and excitement poured out.

"Professor! I really want to be the best at the panel tonight and get the best internship available tonight."

First off, I used the word "best" two times in less than thirty seconds, and second, I was out of breath after saying that one sentence because I was bursting with excitement. In retrospect, Professor Iwa probably knew that I needed to calm down a bit.

"Mr. Sumlin, you're very ambitious, but you want to make sure that you don't let your excitement overwhelm the conversation. I notice in class you can sometimes get too excited."

When he expressed how I could be overwhelming, I instantly wanted to stop him and prove how I wasn't overwhelming. Ironically that would have merely proved his point. At that moment when I wanted to defend my actions and refute what my professor was saying to me, I pondered that maybe he was right. If Professor Iwa could attest to my excitement, then there was a possibility that this was something I needed to work on and improve.

I left his office and I went to the panel later that evening. I went into that situation knowing that no matter what, I would aim to listen rather than speak. That night I met some prominent people and felt good about how I socialized with the panelists.

While mentors can be a source of love and support, they will also tell you things that you might not want to hear. My intent in going to converse with Professor Iwa about the panel was to get insight and feedback about how I could maximize my presence at the event. I knew he would tell me some positive things, but he also said something I needed to hear. Mentors are perfect for that. Just be certain that when you receive constructive criticism from your mentor you are open to the feedback. It took me awhile to get there completely. In my early stages of Morehouse, I thought I knew it all and was never open to constructive criticism. As I matured, I learned some practical ways to deal with criticism while in college.

Stop Your First Reaction

Whenever we are criticized for anything, we all have this innate inclination to be defensive. Most of us believe that we are doing the best we can. When someone challenges our behaviors, ideas or actions, it's hurtful. The mature thing to do is remain calm. Try not to respond. Take a deep breath. Count to ten. Cry in the bathroom if you need to, but whatever you do at that moment, just relax. It's immature to take the criticism personally or respond abrasively.

Listen for Understanding

When someone is criticizing you make it a point to listen with the intent to understand, not to reply. First, this helps you process whatever is being said by the person criticizing you—what he or she is saying may be important. Second, this drastically decreases your opportunity to say something to the other person that could potentially hinder the relationship.

Ask Insightful Questions

Question everything. Asking insightful questions is imperative for personal growth. Make sure that whoever is criticizing you has good intentions. If this person wants to help you and see you grow and develop, he or she will have no problem answering your questions about the feedback. Repeat what this person has said in your questions and get clarity. For example, "I understand that you feel that you want me to engage more in class discussions, is that right?" These questions will show you want to grow, and prove that you are actively listening.

My Favorite Lesson

My mentors have taught me numerous lessons that have helped me achieve my goals. I appreciate all of their wisdom and insight. In class Professor Iwa would always say, "Practice the genius of the AND thinking vs. the tyranny of the OR thinking."

Allow me to demonstrate what this means.

As early as kindergarten, our superiors intentionally program us to accept OR thinking. We learn to view life in dichotomies. A dichotomy is a division or contrast between two things that are represented as being opposed or entirely different. Dichotomies are the essence of OR thinking. As a child I used to tell my classmates that I wanted to be a teacher and a singer. When I would express this to peers, they would respond with OR thinking.

"Chris you should be a teacher or a singer. You have to choose."

This thinking was even projected when it came to simpler subject matter like my favorite color. "I like green and blue," I would say.

"Choose one. It's either one OR the other."

Professor Iwa taught us in class that there was a significant loss to be endured by viewing life with OR thinking. Instead of this notion of seeing life using this or that, he would advocate for AND thinking. Professor would teach us that we had the capacity to do more and be anything we imagined. He preached that we could possess AND thinking.

What would it mean for us if we all decided to embrace AND thinking? I've come to learn that we don't have to give up one part of ourselves for the other. In any situation when we are at a crossroads we should ask ourselves some questions.

What would happen if I did both?

For example: what would happen if I played on the football team and sang in the on-campus acapella group?

Asking ourselves these questions opens the door to reach new heights. My best friend Corbin practices AND thinking. Corbin is a Morehouse graduate from Chicago and we became the best of friends during my sophomore year. I've always known Corbin to possess AND thinking. During his time at Morehouse, Corbin played the violin AND the piano. He studied music AND studied sports. He talked to girls from Clark Atlanta AND Spelman. He was a great friend AND got on my nerves. All jokes aside, possessing AND thinking served him well at Morehouse.

This kind of AND thinking inspires me daily.

It made me a student AND an author.

A blogger AND a YouTuber.

I'm really funny AND good-looking.

The mentoring I got from Professor Iwa helped shape this thinking.

College has its ups and downs, but one way to lessen the burden is to have great mentors to help you along the way. These individuals can help you develop further and achieve more if you are willing to try. I hope you find a supportive mentor during your college experience who will assist in elevating you to becoming the person you desire to be.

<u>WAYS TO DEAL</u>

When Looking For a Mentor

- Find someone you personally and professionally admire
  - ○ Your mentor should be someone you actually like and enjoy being around. It makes the relationship easier to maintain.

- Find someone who has actually achieved something of value
  - ○ A mentor is different from a big brother or big sister. If your mentor has less than three years of experience in your field, he or she is probably more of a peer than a mentor—there's a big difference.

- Find someone you can trust
  - ○ Be very clear with your intentions and definitions of what you want your mentor to be. Do your best not to mix business and pleasure. Keep your mentor relationship professional and respectful at all times.

When You Are Someone's Mentee

- Be someone worth mentoring
  - ○ We all have limited time, and no one wants to spend time working with someone who offers minimal to no return on investment. If you are looking for a mentor,

be a person of value in your field and someone will seek you out, recognizing the value you'll bring to his or her network.

- Be honest
  - ○ No one wants to waste time on people who are lying about what their aspirations are, or who they want to be in the world. Always be very up-front and honest with your mentor about what you are trying to accomplish.
- Listen and work
  - ○ Whenever someone takes the time to give you sound advice, listen and put his or her words to work. If your mentor gives you advice that you don't actually want to take, this person shouldn't be your mentor.

⑧

SECURE THE BAG

"Stay focused and secure your bag, because they want you to fail and they don't want us to win."

—DJ Khaled

As you work your way through college, you will inch closer to the coveted graduation date and hopefully a full-time job opportunity. When people are asked why go to college, the usual answer is to secure a good-paying job. It should go without saying that earning a college degree drastically increases your chances of gaining employment. According to a report from the Center on Education and the Workforce at Georgetown University, of the 11.6 million jobs created after the Great Recession, 8.4 million went to those with at least a bachelor's degree. Another 3 million went to those with associate degrees or some college education.

A college education is a great way to improve your chances of getting a job, but what else? What else can you do to increase your chances of standing out amongst your peers? What can you do during your time in college to assist with the job search later? If you're asking yourself these questions, I have one answer: internships.

Internships are imperative to having a successful tenure in college. At Morehouse, I was lucky enough to secure employment and internships. These opportunities allowed me to grow professionally for my career, as well as network. When dealing with college and all there is to offer, an internship during your undergraduate career will help prepare you for the real world and job market.

The first major internship I held was at 20th Century Fox in Los Angeles during my sophomore year summer. At Fox I was an intern in the Audience Strategy Department, which taught me a lot about television and film. I learned of the internship opportunity from one of my professors who encouraged me to apply. It should be noted that one of the most overlooked ways to gain an internship opportunity is to ask professors if they know anyone who might be looking for interns.

College professors are experts in their fields. Many of them possess doctorate degrees and have deep connections in their designated fields. Because of the experiences that they have, many teachers know working professionals who can help you gain momentum in the early stages of your career.

My internship with Fox was an experience I will never forget. I secured the internship after my sophomore year at Morehouse.

My professor saw that I was an active student, constantly engaging in class and had a passion for television. When I went to him to ask about an internship in Los Angeles, it was easy for him to recommend me to his professional peers. I proved to him that I was worthy of an internship and he knew that I would not let him down.

After my professor gave my name to his former colleagues at Fox, they asked about my resume. Resumes are such an important piece of the securing-the-bag process. I understand the process of writing a resume can be challenging and confusing. It can also be hard to stand out when recruiters and hiring managers receive hundreds of resumes for internships and entry-level roles. When a company is looking to fill a role or position, they don't have the time to look over each resume thoroughly. I read online that the average hiring manager reviews a resume for an average of six seconds when looking for a candidate. With that said, you never want to miss an opportunity because of a simple error. Here are some mistakes you want to avoid when writing your resume.

IRRELEVANT WORK EXPERIENCE

One of the best ways candidates hinder their chances for a role is filling in their resumes with irrelevant work experience. When applying to any job, always make sure that the experiences you include on your resume fit the position for which you are applying.

Before submitting your resume to any kind of opportunity, read over the job description. See if you have work experience that reflects the description of the job you want. The closer you can get your resume to the description of the offered role, the higher your chances of being a match for that position.

HOBBIES SECTION

No one cares about your hobbies. That section on your resume can be used for another header. Never include hobbies that don't directly correlate to the job for which you are applying. Instead of a "Hobbies" section, try including an "Interests" section where you express your interests that match the application. For example, if you are applying to work for E! News, it would not hurt to list "pop culture" as one of your interests in that section.

DELETE YOUR REFERENCES SECTION

Any time an employer wants to speak to references they will ask. There is no need to include this section on your resume. You don't even need to put "references upon request" at the bottom of the document. That statement takes away from space that you can use for something else.

"I" "MY" OR "WE"

A resume should never include personal pronouns. Pronouns

should not be included in your document at all. It is already understood that everything on your resume is a reflection of your experiences. Stating, "We conducted research" or, "I implemented strategies," etc., makes your resume look amateur and very weak.

AN UNPROFESSIONAL EMAIL ADDRESS

Always aim to use your campus email address on your application. You should never use emails like Rihannastan77@yahoo.com or MattyGDaddy@yahoo.com. If those are the only email addresses you have, create another one to use strictly for job applications.

OLD FONT USAGE

The days of Times New Roman 12-point font are over. There are so many cool, modest and creative fonts you can use to stand out in a pile of resumes. Keep it professional but aim to use different fonts that allow you to stand out and be noticed.

TENSE ISSUES

When describing your work experience, always make sure you use the appropriate tense for each experience. If you are presently working at a company, make sure all of your bullets are in the present tense. There are so many people who regularly update their resumes and forget to change the tense of their experiences. Be mindful of this.

SYMMETRICAL FORMAT

It is imperative that your resume is always neat and symmetrical. Symmetry is important in art, creating buildings, and is even used to help beauty campaigns sell makeup. A symmetrical resume should be balanced in the way that the content is laid out on the page. Your words shouldn't be bunched together or unevenly distributed. Resumes can be very complicated documents to format, especially when using templates. Do your best to take your time and configure your document until it is fully balanced.

I implemented these ideas when I created my resume. It was polished and I sent it over. After the team at Fox reviewed my resume, they were impressed and insisted that we discuss the internship further over the phone.

Social Capital

As a first-generation college student, I had no idea how much impact social capital could have when trying to secure employment. What I have come to understand is that when employers are looking for potential candidates for internships or jobs, they hire who they know and who they can trust. While in college, always make sure you aim to be professional and liked by your professors and peers. A reputation for hard work and good character will make you memorable and make it easy for those who know you to recommend you for opportunities.

Everyone knows someone somewhere, and people are always looking for talented candidates for a job. When someone in your network hears of a job or opportunity for which you may be a good fit, you want to be one of the first people in his or her mind. With that said, meet all kinds of people and always be clear about what your aspirations are. So many people refer to this as networking and do it all wrong. Here are some tips for meeting people effectively when looking for employment.

BE NICE

You may not be the smartest person in the room or the most talented, but who cares? People love a genuine smile and pleasant conversation. Do your best to remember names, have a real interest in what people are saying, and do not forget to smile. Good vibes go a long way. I've been in spaces where I was the worst dressed or least qualified. I always tell myself, some may dress better than me, or talk with more eloquence, but no one will ever beat me in making someone feel good.

Everyone who dreams of being successful should possess networking skills. It may be intimidating at first, but the reward is greater than the risk. Next time you hit a networking event I hope these tips come to mind and you knock it out of the park.

FOLLOW UP

The only way to cultivate a relationship is through time and communication. There have been so many instances when I have had a phenomenal conversation with a young professional, but never followed up with him or her. Even though an initial interaction may be good, if I don't make an effort to maintain the relationship it will fall flat. Any time you meet someone who may be able to assist with your career:

- Contact them the next day
- Remind them of the interaction you shared
- In the future contact them every month or two to keep the relationship healthy
- THINK PEOPLE, NOT POSITIONS

A common mistake many of us make is feeling we need to build a connection with the most powerful person in the room. When you're at networking events, connect to people for who they are and not what they do.

We never know who the next Bill Gates will be. It's a lot easier to connect with people at the beginning of their careers than at the pinnacle. We all have people in our lives who are insanely innovative, perfectly punctual and terrifically talented. Make it a point to network with these individuals. It should go without saying that if they are the hard workers of today, they will probably be the game changers of tomorrow. Even if they don't become influencers, these will be interesting relationships. Stay woke.

WATCH YOUR BODY LANGUAGE

A study at UCLA showed that only 7% of communication is based on actual words. For the rest, 38% comes from tone of voice, and the remaining 55% comes from body language. A key to becoming a master networker is learning how to be conscious of the 55% of your communication. When you have the opportunity to meet someone in person, practice precise body language.

- Try to smile
- Never fold your arms
- Stand tall and firm
- PROVIDE VALUE

Everyone has something they are skilled at doing. Any skills that you have while being a student can be of value to someone, somewhere at a company. I've met so many people solely because I write, I'm good at reviewing resumes, or because I'm wickedly good-looking. Whatever your skill or talent, utilize it and make it known. When you can add value to someone's network, it makes it easier to create a healthy professional relationship.

To prepare for my phone interview with FOX, I looked over the job description sent to me. I understood that I was going to be an intern in a department called Audience Strategy. Of course, I had no knowledge of Fox, Audience Strategy, or even what exactly an audience strategist was, but I made it my business to find out. I not only read my job description, but I researched how long the department had been around, news articles published about Fox, as well as strategies I could implement during my internship that could help the team.

In the midst of my research, I hadn't received the job yet. Some may feel that it was a little ambitious to do that level of research, but it did, in fact, help. At the time of my interview, I was 100% ready to articulate my findings. I vividly remember having my notebook in front of me with notes, a Wikipedia page on Fox, and the job description for the position all on hand.

The interview went very well because I prepared. I had done the research, studied it enough to articulate what I wanted to say, and I spoke with a lot of confidence. I was not nervous for the interview—not because it wasn't a big opportunity—but because I knew I was prepared. My preparation and feeling of confidence outweighed my nervousness and anxiety. After the interview was over, I made sure I asked the interviewers some questions that I wanted to be answered, and that was all. After the phone interview, there was a period of a few weeks when I did not hear anything. I was aware that my performance was strong in my interview, but I didn't hear anything for a while. Day after day I would check my email to see if I had overlooked an email from the team. I asked my professor if he had heard anything. But for a while there was nothing. After about three weeks I finally got the email from the HR team at Fox informing me that I got the internship.

Weeks before my internship, I took a bus trip from Atlanta to Columbus, Ohio to return home from Morehouse. This trip back home was at the conclusion of my sophomore year, and I knew that I was not coming back to Morehouse until next fall. For this bus trip I packed everything I could into a huge suitcase. To ensure I was filling my luggage to its capacity, I used Space Bags to minimize my clothes. I watched YouTube videos that helped me fold my clothes more efficiently, and stuffed that luggage to the best of my ability. As life would have it, during my bus trip to Ohio, my luggage went missing.

In retrospect, I understand where I went wrong. Before getting on that bus to head to Ohio, I remember handing my luggage to the bus driver. The luggage was heavy, and I never checked to ensure that it was placed on the bus. I merely handed it over, saw it was put in a line to be put on the bus, and I ran to secure my seat. If you learn anything from this book, please remember: ALWAYS MAKE SURE YOUR LUGGAGE GETS ON THE BUS.

I tell you this luggage story during this chapter because following that fiasco, as you know, I had an internship at Fox in this same summer. Once I was offered the internship and accepted, I understood I would have to figure out what I would wear. Fashion expression is important always, but especially on a job or internship where the goal is to be taken seriously. I knew going into Fox that I wanted to not only work my best, but look my best too. Unfortunately, I only had two pairs of jeans and a T-shirt to do so.

The weekend before I was headed to LA for my internship at Fox, my parents took me to get some quick clothes to wear in the office. At this point, I had a flight to pay for, housing to secure, and numerous expenses to prepare for the internship. Where was I going to go to buy some professional clothes? My parents took me to Target. At Target my father made it a point to tell me to get the essentials. For me, those essentials were polos, slacks, shoes, and belts. I was able to get all of these items for less at Target. I wasn't the most high fashion intern when I got to Fox, but I was professionally dressed and confident.

Your clothes speak for you before you get to say anything. I know that sucks, but it's the truth. After you work hard, network, and get your internship, make sure you have these essential items in your closet to wear during your internship so you can be professionally dressed too.

For Young Men

- Slacks in grey, black, and brown
- Two belts, one black, and one brown

- Two pairs of shoes, one black, and one brown
- Button-up collared shirts to match your slacks and shoes

When getting dressed make sure your belts match your shoes and your clothes are always ironed.

My dad said when getting dressed for a professional setting it's important to be more modest than flashy. Refrain from wearing Gucci belts, Easter Sunday colors, and patterns. When getting dressed for your internship, try to aim more for solid colors and simple patterns. This preference was advice that my father gave me; I hope it works for you too.

For Young Ladies

- Solid black pantsuit
- Black slacks
- Black heels
- Solid-color cardigans
- Beautiful blouses

Ladies, you have way more options than men. You can wear pants some days, skirts the other, just make sure whatever you wear is professional and comfortable. Remember to shy away from items that are too revealing or could be inappropriate for the workplace.

As you secure the bag in your internship, understand that each situation is different. When you go to your gig, study what everyone else is wearing and make it your own. Try to find one or two superiors in your department and monitor how they dress. Implementing the proper style technique from those who are admirable at work will increase your chances for success at your internship.

After my trip to Target with my parents and my flight to LA, it was time to start my internship. For my first day at Fox I wore a blue button-up with brown shoes, a brown belt, and navy slacks. I felt that I was going to do well just because I was dressed for the part.

My first day at the office, I introduced myself to the staff. When I met my supervisor for my internship she acknowledged that I was well dressed. This small compliment assured me that my internship at Fox was going to be great.

My time at Fox was impactful. I learned a lot about marketing TV, life in Los Angeles and how television was created. I truly thought that my Fox internship was a dream come true. I did a good job, made a good impression on my supervisor, but I did make one mistake that taught me a valuable lesson.

I worked at Fox during the summer of 2015, and during this season Fox was launching a new show called *Knock Knock Live*. As an assignment I had to watch the show so I could have an informed opinion on what Fox was doing that year. I didn't like the show. It seemed inauthentic and unfocused to me.

One day while at work, I was casually talking to one of my colleagues (for the purposes of this book we will call her Erica). Erica was not an intern and had been working at Fox for a few years. I liked Erica; she kept me on my A-game and used to give me unsolicited advice whenever she felt I needed it. After lunch, Erica and I had a small conversation.

"How's your lunch, Chris?" she asked.

"It was good; I love having lunch here. I get to see so many great people I can be like when I grow up."

She laughed.

"What do you want to do after college?"

At the time I hadn't given much thought to exactly what I wanted to do after Morehouse, outside of my talk show host aspiration, which I was still ashamed of. I was not sure how to answer, but I tried.

"Well, I would love to be a reality star and have my own show like Kim Kardashian."

"Like Kim Kardashian?" she jokingly asked. "Well you're no Kim K. I don't know who would watch that."

We both laughed. I knew her joke wasn't ill intentioned so I decided to throw one back.

"I bet my show would be more successful than that disaster of a show *Knock Knock*."

I immediately started laughing, but this time I was laughing alone.

"Hey, kid, there's a lot of hardworking people right on this floor who worked to make sure that show did its best. Don't make jokes like that; it's not cool."

The entire mood of the conversation shifted.

Luckily I wasn't fired, but I still learned a good lesson. I learned to be cognizant and careful of my conversation while at work. As college students and interns, if we want to succeed it's imperative that we be extra careful about what we say and how we say it.

Following that interaction, I was more aware of how I said things and even what I joked about to others. I never wanted to miss any opportunity because someone didn't want to be around me or was unsure of what I would say.

As you work to secure your bag and excel in your internship, be careful what kind of jokes you make. We live in a society where one wrong statement or tweet could cost you your job. Stay away from jokes that are homophobic, racist, misogynistic, patriarchal, or could in any way be offensive to anyone. Most notably, stay away from jokes that disrespect or offend your colleagues' work or efforts. If you don't know how to be funny without offending people, then don't crack any jokes at all.

Internships are coveted, and there is more demand for them than supply. If you are ever given a chance to intern with a company, do not blow it or stifle your chances for success because of a tasteless joke.

This lesson can also be applied to social media. Many employers frequent the social media accounts of their potential candidates. During your job search and after you accept a position always be careful of what you post on the internet. Every picture, tweet, and post you create speaks about your character and lifestyle. Do your best to resist the urge to say offensive things while online.

Naturally, we're humans and we are not going to get it right every single time. There will be moments when we make mistakes. I didn't mean any harm when I made that crack about *Knock Knock*; I was trying to clap back. Ironically, *Knock Knock* was canceled after airing just two episodes. Maybe I was right about *Knock Knock* not being a good show, but I was wrong in how I said it.

Maya Angelou notably said, "When you know better, you do better." Luckily I know better now and can tell you this story, so you won't make the same mistake I did.

These ideas will help you secure the bag. If you heed each section of my story, I'm sure your chances of snagging an internship will significantly improve. Following that summer at Fox I came out of that internship ready to take on my junior year with all this new knowledge and wisdom. I can say with confidence that interning with Fox that summer placed me further ahead of the curve. Remember these stories and secure the bag. I look forward to hearing about the internships and ideas you will learn from while you take your journey.

⑨

JAMIL: THE TRUE FRIEND

"Friendship is the hardest thing in the world to explain. It's not something you learn in school. But if you haven't learned the meaning of friendship, you really haven't learned anything."
—Muhammad Ali

In 2013 the rapper Drake released a song titled, "No New Friends." The lyrics to the song preach notions of keeping the same friends around. The song was a smash hit, becoming a Top 40 hit on the Billboard Hot 100. I think the song was such a hit because many people truly believe that keeping the same friends is the key to a successful life. In college new friends are a given. At Morehouse I made a new friend in the strangest way.

During my junior year at Morehouse I had my own dorm room. I stayed on the fourth floor of Mays Hall in room 417. At the time, the fourth floor of Mays was filled with some of the most ambitious men of my class. During Student Government election season, half of the floor was running for elected offices. It was nothing for me to head to my room and see a group of guys engaging in a deep dialogue. Some days respectability would be the topic of discussion, some days girls and their impact on black masculinity, and other days we would discuss the latest football game. Staying on the fourth floor of Mays helped propel my social skills.

One of the aspects I loved about staying in room 417 was that people always stopped by to say hello. I had a speaker system, lots of cool books, and highly decorated walls. I loved keeping my door open and socializing. One night I was hanging with one of my Spelman sisters, Alexandra. Alex was so cool; she was smart, compassionate, and very driven. We connected during a class I was taking at Spelman for my short-lived drama minor. Alex and I took a History of Theatre class together that I really enjoyed. Following our class together that day, Alex insisted that we hang out and talk.

That night, I walked over to Spelman to pick up Alex. We walked around the AUC, smiling and conversing with people, being our usual social selves. Prior to us hanging out I had decorated my room and wanted Alex to come see it. Alex and I are both very spiritual; I wanted her to see how I had transformed my entire room into a vision board. She was excited to see my room and I was anxious to show her, so we left and headed to Morehouse. Once we walked into Mays Hall, it was the typical Mays Hall scene. There were individuals from all different AUC schools in the lobby, enlightening conversation on every staircase, and laughter coming from almost every room. As we made our way up to the fourth floor, Alex and this guy had a brief interaction. They noticed one another but both seemed too shy to speak.

I was unsure what had just happened so we continued upstairs.

"Did you see that guy who was just staring at me?" Alex asked.

Alex must have peeped the guy looking at her because she was interested.

"He's kinda cute," she added.

"Well why don't you go and try to talk to him," I replied.

"Cause that's awkward. I don't even know his name."

Most people I had interacted with were very friendly, and I knew that she and that guy would have good conversation if only she was open to speaking up.

"Well whatever happens, happens. I'm sure I'll see him again," Alex said.

Following our time in my room it was getting late, so I insisted on walking Alex back to Spelman.

It had been a long day and I was exhausted, but as I returned to my room I noticed a note on my floor. I always kept my room clean, so I could tell immediately if anything was ever out of place. When I picked up the note I saw it read: "Yo Bro! This is Jamil from 305. Your friend is cute. Give her my number so we can talk. I know this is childish but Idc. Have her hit me up."

This was the first time in a while I had seen a handwritten love note. On one side I was humored that this guy would write a letter to meet a girl, on another side I was impressed with his confidence to make such a bold move.

On the note was Jamil's number, so after consulting Alex I began planning for the perfect time to invite them to my room—together.

That weekend I decided to invite friends over for some fun. I invited a couple of girls over, my best friend Corbin, Alex of course, and most importantly, Jamil. I didn't remember what Jamil looked like, I had never heard of him before around campus, had no idea who I was texting when I invited him to come up to my room. Jamil could have been the janitor for all I knew, because I barely got a glimpse of him when we passed on the stairway. Once all my friends were in my room hanging, I knew that I had to invite Jamil up.

I sent him a text: "Hey Bro, It's Chris from room 417, myself and some friends are hanging in my room and you're more than welcome to come and join."

At this point I was putting myself out there to hang and he could either accept or decline. After a few minutes of uncertainty I got a text that said, "Alright bet."

We were all still in my room listening to music and having fun when I got a knock on the door. Checking through my peephole I knew it was Jamil. I opened the door.

"Hey man, come on in," I said with a smile.

When he walked in, all the girls in the room instantly took notice and were intrigued. The night went well. I considered myself to be a pro at getting to know people and making them feel comfortable, so I began my questioning.

"So man, where are you from?"

"Chicago."

"Nice, Corbin's from Chicago too. What's your major?"

"Biology."

He replied to each question I asked with a one-word answer and he spoke with such a deep voice. I assumed he wasn't friendly and wasn't enjoying my company. Later that night, we went to a party as a whole squad. Alex and Jamil had finally met in person and started having excellent conversation; everything went pretty decent. I saw that they were getting closer and that my work was done.

The next morning I received a text from Jamil: "Thanks for last night bro, your friend is really cool."

What I thought was just a crush between a guy and one of my friends became so much more. Once Jamil started hanging out with my friends and me more often he began coming out of his shell and we officially became a squad.

Corbin and Jamil bonded over the fact that they were both from Chicago. Jamil and Alex's friendship began to deepen. Before I could recollect what had happened, Jamil, Alex, Corbin and I were hanging out every weekend. There were times when Alex was busy, and we would hang with my Spelman sister, Maya, and her friends instead. Everyone I brought Jamil around enjoyed how laid back and cool he was. We continued to hang out all the way up until Homecoming season. At this point, we were officially a squad.

One night the entire squad went out. After a night of turning up, we all went back to our rooms. But Jamil, like a real Man of Morehouse, offered to walk Alex back to Spelman. I was able to go back to my room and get some rest. Shortly after we separated I was in my room and I got a knock on my door. I didn't know who it was. I knew that I didn't have any music on and I wasn't doing anything wrong. It couldn't be the RA. I opened the door, and it was Jamil. I thought, *Oh no, he and Alex must have fought or something. What can he possibly want after we all had a good night and everyone is tired?*

He walked in.

"Hey man, did you have a good time, didn't we have fun?"

"Yeah man, that's what I wanted to talk to you about."

I knew the bad news had to be coming. He took a seat and began to speak.

"I just wanted to say thanks for everything. You've been a good friend since the first time I came to your room, thank you."

I was floored. The whole time I suspected that Alex was his only goal, and if they didn't work out he and I wouldn't be friends simply because I assumed he didn't care for having me around.

"Yeah man, no problem. It's fun having us all hang."

"Yeah bro, we stay lit. Well that's it. I'll let you get some rest."

We shook hands, and he left.

Following that Homecoming week, Jamil has never left my side. To this day we are still good friends, and he teaches me invaluable lessons that I will always cherish. This random occurrence of events shows how spontaneously a friendship can start in college. There are five main very important characteristics that I believe Jamil embodies as a friend. These five principles are the kind of characteristics that we all should look for when trying to make friends, especially in college.

1. DEPENDABILITY

True friends will always be there for you when you need them. Whether you just had a major family crisis and need an ear to vent to, or you're out of money and need five dollars for laundry. No matter what, a true friend will have no problem getting his or her hands dirty and fighting in the sand with you. They will always do their absolute best to make sure you have what you need, and they will support you no matter what. The best way to test true friends is to hit them with a crisis that you know they have the resources to help you with, and then see how they react. If someone is a true friend he or she will assist. If this person is not a true friend, he or she will resist and won't help you. Always appreciate the ones who have your back in a crisis, and those who don't make you feel bad about asking for or receiving help.

2. ACCOUNTABILITY

A true friend will always hold you accountable. I can always count on Jamil to get on me about my eating and drinking habits.

Every day he will call me reminding me, "Chris, did you hit the gym?"

"Chris what did you eat today? You know health is wealth."

I hate him for always holding me accountable, but I know that it's all in the name of friendship. Share your goals with your friends and see if they hold you accountable enough to help you achieve them. A true friend will never let you look less than your best, act a fool or wander off from your goals. Real friends bring out the best in each other by holding each other accountable.

3. TRUSTWORTHINESS

The best characteristic of a true friend is trustworthiness. When meeting new friends, always ask yourself:

"Can I trust this person?"

"Is my back covered?"

"Would my friend ever do something to dishonor me?"

True friends do their best to honor you. They will talk positively behind your back and won't tell your secrets. A true friend is one you can trust with your secrets, your resources, and most importantly, your heart.

4. HONESTY

A true friend will always keep it honest with you. When in college, there will be people who won't care about you enough to tell you the truth, especially when it hurts.

5. GENEROSITY

True friends will always do everything in their power to give you whatever they have. If you have a real friend, reflect on how much time, energy, and resources this person gives you in a week. We are all busy, we all have expenses and a lot going on, but the ones who make an effort to give you the best they've got, those are your real friends.

I appreciate all of the great friends I made during my time at Morehouse. I particularly appreciate Jamil for allowing me to share this story. He's still not as loud as me, we don't listen to the same music, and he's vegan so we can't even bond over Fried Chicken Wednesday. What I can say, is that I have never met a more loyal person. It's crazy, because had Alex and I not walked up the stairs at that exact time, I probably would have never met Jamil. While in college, keep an open mind. Do your best to navigate through your college campus with the intention of finding and being a good friend. If someone leaves a note under your door to get at one of your friends, read it and honor it. That same person could end up becoming one of your truest friends.

WAYS TO DEAL

When New Friends Approach You

- Accept them with an open heart
- Invite them to your functions and give them the chance to be friends
- Don't rush the friendship
    - Building friendships takes time. Each moment you have with another person is a chance to inch closer and closer to him or her becoming your true friend.

When You Have a Friend Who Isn't Being a True Friend

- Communicate how you feel
    - No one can read minds. If you have a problem with the way someone is treating you, address the situation.

When You Have a Good Friendship

- Choose compassion over cynicism
    - Care more about doing what is right instead of always being right.

- Embrace quality over quantity
  - Make sure you surround yourself with good people you enjoy being around. That may mean you have less friends, but it is greater to have a few good friends than a hundred bad ones.

- Don't let technology be your only means of communication
  - Life changes and people change. The way to keep up with the changes of people is not through Facebook or occasional text conversations. Get in the same room as your friends and put effort into the actual friendship.

(10)

THE A-WAY

"You can want success all you want, but to get it, you can't falter. You can't slip, you can't sleep. One eye open, for real, and forever."
—Jay-Z

Making good grades in college is different from making good grades in high school. College work requires more attention, time, and focus. The classwork is more rigorous, there are more distractions, and no one's there to make you go to classes. Now, I'll be honest; I could have been a stronger student in college. The highest GPA I ever received while at Morehouse was a 3.49, which I earned my last semester during my final year. While at Morehouse there were some classes in which I excelled and received A's. There was a time when I dropped a class and there were classes when my goal was to simply get a passing grade.

I know that I could have done better. Throughout my time in

undergrad I learned lots of useful tricks that would have helped me make higher grades if I had known them before I started college.

Show Up

Woody Allen once said, "Showing up is 80% of success." It should go without saying that to succeed in any class, at least try to attend. One of the classes I earned an A in during my time at Morehouse was a course called Buyers Behavior. The course was taught by a brilliant woman named Professor McGriff. She knew her stuff and expected all her students to come to class knowing their stuff too. The course material was not too heavy; it was a marketing class. We would evaluate different marketing strategies by various companies and discuss them. I succeeded in that class. I did well because when I came to class, I showed up.

Showing up does not simply mean just coming to class and being present—you also need to have a presence. Being present in class is the act of being in the geographic location where the class is taking place. This practice of coming to class is the bare minimum. Having a presence in a class is when you are fully engaged and actively participating in the course. This approach is when you not only show up with your body, but you also show up with your mind and soul.

Buyers Behavior was a class in which I did well because I had a presence during each lecture. I came to class dressed professionally, which made me feel good as well as actively engaged in dialogue with the professor. I credit the A that I got in the class because I was focused and made sure I had good contributions to the class discussions.

Collaborate

Another class I received an A in was a course titled Hollywood, Politics and Power, which was one of my major courses. This class was another one that required class participation for students' success. Along with class participation, we had three real assignments throughout the entire semester: a midterm, a final, and a presentation. In my experience, this was how a lot of my college courses were built. In high school, there are a plethora of opportunities to turn in little homework assignments here, in-class work there, and your grade is always changing. For me, that was not the case in college. Most of the classes were set up with minimal assignments and mostly exams.

In Hollywood Politics and Power, I did well on my presentations, but I had to work extra hard on the class midterm and final exam. For this course we were given a study guide from our professor. After reviewing the study guide it was clear that I needed the required textbook for the class, which I never purchased. The midterm study guide consisted of mostly short-answer questions and essays. I was overwhelmed by how much knowledge we needed just to complete the study guide. Leading up to the exam, I talked with some of my classmates about the exam, and we decided that if we wanted to do well on the test, we should work together. This collaboration allowed us to teach each other and answer each other's questions.

When I took the exam I was confident knowing that I had not only studied hard by myself, but also collaborated with my peers to ensure my competence on the coursework. I earned an A on that exam and inevitably made an A in the course. Academic collaboration is an excellent way to make A's in college. Our professors can be effective in teaching the material, but it helps a ton to have a peer explain the material as well to complement what the professor went over in class.

When dealing with college and trying to make good grades, don't be afraid to collaborate with your peers. There is never a class every student is failing; that is highly unlikely. Consequently there is always a student who will make sure that he or she will earn the A. Do your best to make it a point to find someone in class you know is doing well, or even ask the professor if there is an assigned tutor for the course. Collaborating with a student to make good grades is not only a way to earn A's, but meet new people as well.

Know Your Professors

One of the biggest keys to succeeding in college in any respect is maintaining good relationships with everyone you meet. Hands down, the best relationships to prioritize are those with your professors. Sometimes as students we forget that educators were students too. They got to where they are by excelling in their coursework enough to earn a career in education. Many of the professors I had the pleasure of learning from at Morehouse had doctorate degrees. They had a deep passion for learning, and more importantly, teaching. One thing I know for sure is that there is no better professor than one who has an evident passion for what he or she is teaching.

In college, your professors will enjoy answering your questions after class and in their offices during office hours. When you receive your syllabi at the beginning of your courses make sure you highlight your professors' contact information and intend to use it. I could tell countless stories of how I built up a good relationship with a professor and how that allowed me to succeed.

During my last semester at Morehouse I took a history class that taught the history of Morehouse. I was filling my transcript with elective hours and thought that this class would provide me with an easy A. If there is one lesson I learned about college life, it is that there is no such thing as an easy A.

The History of Morehouse College course was taught by Dr. Marcellus Barksdale. I had the honor of being in the final course that Dr. Barksdale taught at Morehouse before retiring. I remember having a brief conversation with one of my classmates about the course.

"Dr. Barksdale is retiring, you know he's going to give everyone A's this semester. This class will be a breeze," he said.

He couldn't have been more wrong. Dr. Barksdale wasn't one of the longest serving faculty members in the history of Morehouse for nothing; he had no plan to end his time at Morehouse on any note less than the best.

The course was fun. There were some of the biggest personalities at Morehouse in the class. We had candid discussions and I literally used to get sad when it came time for the class to end because we would have so much fun. The fun quickly ended when it came time for our midterm. The test was 100 questions, all multiple choice, covering all of the history of Morehouse we had discussed in class. I never understood why people enjoy multiple choice tests over short-answer; the objectivity always gave me lots of anxiety. I remember taking that midterm, having not properly prepared for the course and completely bombing.

The test consisted of questions like, "Was Morehouse founded in 1879, 1867, 1857 or 1869?" It was one of those tests that showed whether or not you knew the material, and there was no way around it.

Once it came time for Dr. Barksdale to return the test, I knew I had failed. I had every intention of keeping my test face down and running out of the room after he handed it to me. At the end of class he handed back the test.

"Mr. Sumlin?"

I went up to receive my test and prepared for my dash out of the room. Instead, Dr. Barksdale whispered to me after handing me my poor test.

"Can you wait one second for everyone to leave? I want to talk to you after class."

I knew he wanted to discuss my failed exam. I was so embarrassed. All I wanted to do was run fast and avoid the reality of what happened regarding my exam.

Dr. Barksdale and I headed out of the class together and discussed my failed test.

"Mr. Sumlin—what happened? You were one of my most vocal students in class, how did you fail?"

I sighed in shame.

"I don't know, Professor. I think I was just too confident and didn't take the test seriously enough."

"Well you know this is a serious course. You need to give it your best. You're too smart to make those kinds of grades."

I had shown up to class and proven to Dr. Barksdale that I had the capacity to do well, and because of this he knew I was underperforming.

"Yes sir, I understand," I humbly stated.

"Very well then. If you have any questions or need some help feel free to stop by my office and ask for help. Don't just sit there and fail, knowingly."

After that conversation with Dr. Barksdale I waited for him to get into the elevator and then I dashed out of the building before he could catch me. I took his advice. I knew that in order to succeed I had to up my game and ask for help if I needed it.

Get to know your professors and ask for help if you need it. Like Dr. Barksdale said, "Don't fail, knowingly."

If you find yourself unsure in a class or need more help, talk to your professor and go to his or her office during office hours.

Following that exam, I studied a lot harder in the later weeks of the course. If there was ever something I didn't understand in class, I would come early and Dr. Barksdale and I would discuss it. I was also never too prideful to send him an email or go to his office. I built a relationship and rapport with Dr. Barksdale that set the foundation for me to succeed in his class.

After talking with Dr. Barksdale and taking his class more seriously, I aced the final exam and earned a B in his class. I credit this grade not to my academic ability, but because I had a strong interest in the class and an incredible relationship with my professor.

WAYS TO DEAL

When You Find Yourself Struggling In a Class

- Look for students in the class who may be doing well and try to collaborate
  - If you decide to work in a group with your peers, come to the study group with notes and specific questions.
  - Never decide to meet with a classmate unprepared.

- Go to office hours and talk with your professor
  - Building a relationship with a professor significantly increases your chances of doing well in a course.
  - Be candid and honest with your professors; it is their job to help and assist you in a course.

- Keep an open-mind approach
  - If you are given some advice from a peer or your professor about how to prepare for a class, take it with an open mind. Don't be stubborn when it comes to different ways of studying.

TIME MANAGEMENT AND PRIORITIES

"The key is not to prioritize what's on your schedule, but to schedule your priorities."

—Stephen Covey

My biggest accomplishment while in school was writing my first book, *Dealing with This Thing Called Life*. I had such a good time writing it and an even better time going around campus trying to sell it. Writing the book was not something that was required for a class, or something someone made me do; it was something I wanted to do.

I'll never forget the day I decided I wanted to write a book. I was sitting at home with my mother watching television during the summer of my sophomore year. It was a game show and I was not really paying attention. I sat there, passively gazing at the screen, when I was struck by an epiphany. The entire outline for a book came to me in a flash. The thought was, *Dealing with This Thing Called Life: 12 Chapters, 12 Lessons, 12 Affirmations*. I wasn't thinking of writing a book, nor had I ever dreamed of becoming an author. After changing my major from business to television, my only big dream was that one day I'd have my own talk show and inspire people through television. I always thought of maybe doing a TED Talk, maybe even having a reality show, but I never entertained the idea of becoming an author.

Following my divine epiphany, as I've learned to call it, I knew I had to do something with this idea. This epiphany was unlike anything I had ever felt before. I felt this intense urge to manifest this idea and get started. My mother was in the kitchen making dinner. I felt that if I was going to run this idea by anyone I should run it by her first.

"Mom, I think I want to write a book."

"A book? What made you think of that?" she asked.

I told her how the entire idea came to my mind in an instant.

I said, "I think I wanna write a book and really tell my story."

"I think that would be good, I look forward to reading it."

That was the entire conversation. It was brief but reaffirming. Steve Harvey once said, "Never tell your big dreams to small-minded people." He was right when he said that. I think that had my mother told me I was crazy, I probably would have dismissed the entire notion.

This proposal stayed in the back of my mind for quite some time. I discussed it lightly with some close friends, but I never really pursued the idea. Months went by, and before I knew it I was back at Morehouse for my junior year. After classes had really sunk in, financial aid was handled, and my Mariah Carey posters were on my dorm room walls, the idea came back to me again. It was the strong random flash experience that I'd had at my mother's house, but this time it was more subtle. It was like a voice had spoken to me and reminded me of the moment that took place at my mother's house. I finally understood that this time I needed to actually get started.

On September 7, 2015 I posted a status on Facebook that read, "I'm writing a book. When it's finished and published who's buying it? Show me some love, Facebook. Like this status if you'd buy a book written by Chris Sumlin!"

One thing I love about social media is that once you put an idea out into the world, people take notice and look to see if you're actually going to follow through with what you said. That week of my Facebook announcement status, I got to writing.

What had previously seemed to be an impossible venture now seemed to be manifesting itself. I started with a blank Google Doc file and began slowly chugging through my ideas. The process began with an outline of what stories I wanted to tell. I equipped each story with a necessary lesson I thought my peers would appreciate, then I began writing.

During the time of writing my original manuscript, classes were in session. I never abandoned my schoolwork, I just worked hard to manage my time. I would schedule out how long I would be in the cafeteria, I would budget time for office hours and study time. A major takeaway from this experience was understanding how much time we all have in a day. Each day is equipped with twenty-four hours, nothing more, nothing less. One of my favorite quotes I see floating around the internet is: "You have the same hours in a day as Beyoncé."

The reality is that each one of us is given twenty-four hours in a day. I like to think Beyoncé excels in her ability to manage time effectively to manifest her goals.

Time management is a skill that is imperative for success in college. There are going to be so many things to do. There will be classes, friends, and events on campus that will be overwhelming. The key is to get about the business of managing your time. I'll give you some insight into how my days went during my book writing process.

I would wake up around 5:00 a.m. and write. I knew that none of my friends were morning people and I would be able to work uninterrupted during these peak hours of the morning. The cafeteria opened for breakfast around 7:00 a.m., and I would go there to eat. As I ate breakfast I would read books to double up on my productivity. Not only was I eating the most important meal of the day, I was also reading books regularly to help me stay inspired.

During my junior year I was taught by a Morehouse Man named Avery Williams. Professor Williams used to always tell us in his screenwriting class, "Great writers are great readers. If you want to produce great writing you have to read great work."

I took this statement literally and decided to make reading a daily part of my life. There were also instances when I would need to do laundry. Whenever I had laundry that needed to be done I would put it in during my breakfast hours because I knew no one was awake and I could be very productive. This practice allowed me to eat breakfast, read books, and do laundry all at the same time.

After I ate breakfast, it would be time to prepare for classes. This preparation would consist of getting dressed and studying for class. By this time it would be noon. I would go to my classes and work on schoolwork for the majority of sunlight hours. During the day, my peers were available to help me study and I could send emails to professors if needed. I would work on school and have dinner and prepare for bed that evening. I did this routine for about a month until my first draft manuscript was complete.

College is a great time to create businesses, products, and try new things. Whatever you want to do or create in college is possible. I know from experience that in college, anything is possible. Conversely, I also learned from my journey that nothing at all is possible without priority.

If you do decide you want to write a book, launch a business or start a YouTube channel, you absolutely can. Accomplishing goals like these will take some time management skills that will allow you to work smarter not harder and seize the day.

Busy vs. Productive

There is a huge difference between staying busy and being productive. We all know people who seem to be taking on the world. Whenever you see them they are dressed to a tee, constantly ranting about all of these ventures they are working on, and they are so "busy." These are the ones who scurry from task to task, stay on the phone handling "business" and are "grinding." But when you deeply evaluate the result of their tireless grind and impeccably perfect work ethic you see...nothing. These are the individuals who are busy, not productive.

Productivity begets success naturally. Anyone who has achieved any level of success has done so by maintaining some level of productivity. Productivity looks different on each person. The goal is not to look productive like the aforementioned busy people; the goal is to get results. Your equation for what allows you to be productive may be different from mine. I'm naturally a morning person. I love waking up, enjoying a sunrise, and getting to work. Conversely, I'm not a night person at all. My friends often laugh at me because when we go out, I guarantee you I'm the first one asleep in the Uber on the way home. I don't work well at night. You may be different, you may enjoy the stillness of the night and that works for you. Either way is fine, the goal is productivity.

Important vs. Urgent

During a 1954 speech, former US President Dwight D. Eisenhower quoted Dr. J. Roscoe Miller, president of Northwestern University, when he said: "I have two kinds of problems: the urgent and the important. The urgent are not important, and the important are never urgent." Scholars all over the world have come to know this principle of distinguishing importance and urgency as the "Eisenhower Principle."

The Eisenhower Principle is a perfect strategy to implement to determine what you should do next. While in college recognize the distinction between what is urgent and what is important.

Important activities possess value that will eventually help achieve your goals.

Urgent activities possess value that requires immediate action in order to achieve your goals.

These two distinguished ideas can intersect. There can be ideas that are:

Important and Urgent

These are activities that are important and require immediate attention. In college an example of an important and urgent activity would be studying for an exam you have that week. The results of the exam are important because they affect your grades. The exam is also urgent because you only have so much time to study before you take the exam.

Important but Not Urgent

Important but not urgent tasks are ones that have consequences or may be important to us, but do not require immediate action. For instance, it was very important to me that I finished my book manuscript, but it was not urgent seeing as how I had no concrete deadline in place. There were moments when I would have assignments due that were overwhelming. In order to address the situation, I had to handle my assignments first because the assignments possessed more urgency than my book manuscript.

Neither Important nor Urgent

These are the activities that serve as distractions and should be avoided at all costs. This is where the majority of people spend their time—entertaining activities that are neither important nor urgent. One of my favorite shows out today is *House of Cards*. I thoroughly enjoy the show because of the impeccable writing and plot twists. There were moments during my journey through college when I would binge-watch *House of Cards* all day, neglecting my responsibilities. In my little mind, I may have viewed completing the entire season of *House of Cards* as important and urgent, but in my mature college mind I know that is not the case.

Dealing with college is about maturity and making the best decisions you can that are conducive to your success. Of course you can enjoy your friends, go for drinks, and binge-watch Netflix series. The deciding factor is whether you are entertaining these activities at the expense of achieving your goals.

Make Good Habits

One way to ensure that you are using your time wisely is to make good habits. Modern psychology tells us that it takes twenty-three days to create a habit. Positive habits make being productive easy because it's habitual. Writing my last book was not a burden or something I dreaded doing, because writing became such a habit for me during that time. During my junior year of college I was writing screenplays, blogs, and working on a book. Writing became something that I needed to do daily in order to make good grades and work on my brand. It became nothing for me to sit still in one morning and chug out 3,000 words, because it was a habit.

Whatever it is you want to do in college, make a habit out of it. If you want to lose three pounds like Regina George (for my *Mean Girls* fans), make it a habit to work out. If you want to start a You-Tube channel and create online video content, make it a habit to shoot your shot regularly. Whatever you want to do or create while in college is possible, it just takes priority.

Trade-Offs

The biggest thing we forget as individuals navigating through the world, is that no one has it all. We may be able to post the most wonderful selfies, write the most beautifully articulate Facebook posts, but in reality no one has it all. Oprah once said, "You can have it all. You just can't have it all at once."

In college while you're determining what is important, what's urgent, and making your decisions, you will make sacrifices. While I was writing my book, I easily gained fifteen pounds from always sitting down and writing. I was so focused on writing and blogging that I neglected physical activity. Of course I was reading every Brené Brown book I could get my hands on, and had followed Mark Manson's blog, but I wasn't out playing basketball with my boys in the gym during the evenings.

In retrospect, I'm proud of my decision to write my book and neglect fitness, because that was a choice I consciously made. The choice to write over exercise was a decision that I had to accept. As you decide what you want to do in college, understand that sacrifices will have to be made. The man who attempts to have it all at once, inevitably ends up with nothing.

Do Less

My junior year at Morehouse was the year I left the glee club after two successful runs of being a member. It was that year when I knew that my time in the glee club was distracting me from other passion projects on which I wanted to work. I made the trade-off to leave the glee club and work on my book, website, and YouTube channel. On top of making sacrifices and trading activities for others, you can also simply do less.

Say no to things if they don't serve the vision or plan that you have for yourself. When I was writing my book I was unable to be at every party. I could not turn up every weekend. I decided to turn that down so I could turn up writing. Never be afraid to say no to tasks or activities if they don't help you with your goals.

Stillness

Doing less is something that has particularly helped me stay productive. When we have so much going on in our lives and we're trying to accomplish our goals it can get hard to get still. Stillness is an excellent practice to have when you find yourself getting overwhelmed. There are times when I just need complete silence. This silence consists of no music, no cell phone, and nobody. These moments of stillness allow me to observe my thoughts and relax. Making time for silence and non-motion have truly helped me get centered and back on track toward what I need to do. If there are instances when I struggle with anxiety or feel overwhelmed, I practice stillness and relax.

I sit still, back straight, maybe with my legs crossed, and close my eyes. I begin to breathe deeply. I may only do this for five minutes, but that time of stillness and silence calms me and allows me to get work done more efficiently.

Imperfection

Time management and prioritizing in college is a practice, and as with any practice there will be shortcomings. As I write these very words I still struggle with balancing importance and urgency. You may not get it right every time. The goal is to simply try. Remember, you are completely capable of doing extraordinary work in college.

WAYS TO DEAL

When You Find Yourself Overwhelmed with Tasks

- Find out where you are wasting time
  - Assessing your daily activities and time spent can assist you in making cuts and changes wherever needed.
  - The first step to effective time management is getting an accurate picture of how much time you spend.
- Use time management tools

- There are lots of phone applications such as Google Calendar that can help you structure your day more effectively.

When Evaluating What You Want to Cut Out of Your Day

- Look for return on investment
  - There are some tasks that are fulfilling and rewarding and others that are just draining. Get rid of the tasks that don't return a lot of fulfillment and take a lot of time.

When You Are Looking to Start a New Project

- Establish a routine and stick with it
  - There are some things in life that will arise, but routines greatly increase your chances for productivity.

- Remember: success will require sacrifices
  - Trade-offs are essential to living a balanced life. Understanding the costs of what it takes to achieve your goals will make it less daunting when you find yourself making sacrifices in order to be successful.

  - Learn to say "no" to tasks that don't serve you or your goals.

- Take care of your physical health
  - Sacrificing sleep is never a good way to hack productivity. We need seven to eight hours a night for our bodies and brains to function properly. Make sacrifices but never sacrifice sleep.

(12)

RUN YOUR RACE

"My great mistake, the fault for which I can't forgive myself, is that one day I ceased my obstinate pursuit of my own individuality."

—Oscar Wilde

During my time in college I found myself in competition and comparing myself to others. In a world plagued by "proud to announce" Facebook posts and "Just got the new internship at Goldman" tweets, we often feel the need to compare ourselves to others. It's almost like a game of who can be the best and articulate their experiences the best on the internet. It's a game we all can find ourselves playing; we want to portray the best of ourselves always. We want to show the world that we are snagging the best internships, eating the best meals and going to the best concerts.

I found myself playing this game a lot. During my time in undergrad I would see one of my Facebook friends posting about how he had a great time at brunch, and then I would want to go to brunch and see if I could outdo him. I would witness someone getting a cool internship for the summer, and then I would apply to like thirty jobs just to be in the game and not feel left behind. As I reflect on this unspoken game I would play with others, I find I was good at it. I had pictures with celebrities, pictures of cocktails from No Mas, and internship announcement posts that shook my campus.

Once my senior year came around and it was time to get "a real job," I still had the need to play "the game." As we started getting closer and closer to commencement, it seemed as if everyone was announcing the next venture they would be taking on after their time at Morehouse. Some guys were going abroad to travel to Haiti, others were accepting full-time roles at profitable companies such as SunTrust Bank and Goldman Sachs. I was inspired by these posts and knew I wanted to find myself a cool job too. I was not exactly sure what it was that I wanted to do, but I felt that since I had played the game of being the best, I had to find the best, sexiest, "OMG" job I could find. Day after day, I was updating my LinkedIn account and applying for full-time roles. By the middle of March, I had officially joined the game of trying to find the best job.

I knew that I was going to have job offers flooding in. By this time I had numerous impressive internships on my resume, what I presumed to be the perfect LinkedIn profile, and I also considered myself to be in possession of some pretty good interpersonal skills.

My confidence in playing the game was high because I knew that I would find the best job out there.

As time went by I received no emails, no calls—nothing. It was strange to me how I was unable to even secure an interview. It seemed as if something had blackballed me and prevented my resume from touching the desk of a hiring manager. I consulted with friends, I sought the counsel of my family, and everyone kept telling me the same thing: "Focus on yourself, run your race. It will come together eventually."

I was not used to "eventually." I was used to "instantly." I was spoiled and drunk from the experiences I had in my sophomore and junior years at Morehouse. I was ready to get my sexy job.

After weeks had gone by and nothing was coming my way, I thought maybe there was something else I should be doing.

I once saw a quote on Instagram that said, "Relax and trust the timing of your life." That quote is a mantra that I meditate on daily. As I was in the space of uncertainty regarding what to do about my post-grad life, I began to question what I should do.

"Should I keep applying to jobs?"

"Is it meant for me to graduate, am I going to fail a course?"

"Should I work for myself and launch a consulting company?"

"What's next?"

I was content knowing that whatever was supposed to happen was going to happen.

One weekend changed everything. It was the weekend my Morehouse brother Russell came to Atlanta. Russell graduated a year before I did and was always there for mentorship and support. He's the friend I would call whenever I didn't know what to do because he always had an answer. After Russell graduated from Morehouse in 2016, he enrolled in a master's program at the University of Tennessee in Knoxville. When we would talk, he would always tell me about his experiences in graduate school and how awesome it was. I didn't know too many people in my family with advanced degrees, so for me graduate school was not something on my radar.

During the weekend of Russell's visit, he came over one Saturday morning. We shared some light conversation and laughs until he hit me with the question I didn't want to hear.

"So how are your post-grad plans coming? Are you going to work for Oprah?"

As he asked this question, I was nervous and unsure what to say. I knew that I hadn't heard from the Oprah Winfrey Network or anyone at the time. I knew that I was doing my best, but nothing had worked out yet. I didn't want to feel stupid or lazy, and I didn't know what to say.

"Well…I sent over my resume and applied for a job; I'm hoping to hear back soon," I replied.

Russell was quiet for a minute. Then he asked, "If that doesn't work out, I think you should consider grad school."

He could have told me to apply for the circus and it would have made more sense. I knew absolutely nothing about grad school.

"Huh? You think that's a good move?"

Russell patiently said, "Graduate school could be a good move for you. You're really smart and focused like they are in grad school. You're gonna want to take your skillset and advance it; a graduate program could help you do that."

I paused. I thought to myself, *This could be a good option.*

Following that brief conversation, we began researching grad programs to which I could apply. We looked at all different kinds of schools for about an hour. A week later I made a promise to myself that I would seriously explore the idea of attending grad school. I planned to apply to one grad school. I thought, *If it's meant to be I will get in, and if not, I'll continue on my sexy job search.* I decided that I owed it to myself to at least give it my best try and see what could happen.

When my search began, my intent was simply to find a program that would complement my coursework at Morehouse. I understood that I had a passion for television and would earn a degree in CTEMS, so I wanted something that wouldn't stray too far away from that. This time, I wasn't trying to find the sexiest, "OMG," wow program I could post and brag about, but something that would serve me and my passions.

One day I found myself on the website of Boston University. I had searched "master's degree television" and it brought me to the

BU site. I had never been to Boston University's campus and never heard much about the school besides the fact that it was where Dr. Martin Luther King went to earn his doctorate degree. Martin Luther King was always described to me as Morehouse's most illustrious alum. I thought, *If I can go to Boston after Morehouse like Dr. King, maybe I can do great work as he did.*

Luckily, Boston had a master of science program in television. The program's website stated its mission and vision. As I read over it, it was clear that this program was perfect for me. They had a concentration in their master's program in producing and management, which is what I had always dreamed of learning about. It was evident that if I was going to apply to one graduate program, this was the program. I started working on the application the day I saw the BU website. I told no one; the only individuals I talked to about BU were the staff members I asked for letters of recommendation. I wanted to do as my mantra stated: "Focus on myself and run my race." This decision was for me; it wasn't about posting it or sharing it. This application was about me, my life, and what I wanted to do in the world.

The BU television master's program was under the school of communication. When I was deciding who I wanted to ask about letters of recommendation, I knew that I had to be strategic and find mentors who could really tell my story in the best light. With this in mind, I asked Professor Adisa Iwa, my Introduction to Television professor. I asked Cathy Tyler, the director of strategic communication at Morehouse. Lastly, I asked Elia Sanchez who worked with me at 20th Century Fox in Los Angeles. These three individuals were people with whom I had maintained positive relationships, and their professions would hopefully, strategically, convince the BU admissions office that I was worthy of this program.

I worked really hard on my essays. I knew that I had a passion for writing and understood why I was applying to this specific program. I completed the entire application within a matter of days. I had gathered my letters of recommendation, written two compelling essays, and asked the school to waive my application fee. It had seemed everything was coming together so seamlessly. There was no struggle to complete the application; in my heart I felt like it was right.

Three weeks after I submitted my application I was hanging in my room with another Morehouse brother named Marvin. We were discussing life, goals and trusting in God. It was crazy because as we were having a rather inspiring conversation, I got an email. The email congratulated me on officially being accepted into the Boston University School of Communication as a grad student.

When I read the email I was ecstatic. I got the email on May 1st, less than thirty days away from my Morehouse commencement. After I got the email I told everyone. It felt good knowing that it worked, I believed, and I got accepted, granting my wish of knowing what I was going to do following Morehouse. I never heard back from any jobs, I never got any offers. The only opportunity that wanted me with open arms was this graduate program.

College can be tough. I know from experience that it never gets easier, it only gets harder. You can find relief in knowing that as it gets harder, you'll get stronger. With each chapter and year, there lies a new lesson and a new experience. Follow your path. If I can do it with my ever-present insecurities and inadequacies I know you can too. Run your race well, and live your story. I look forward to hearing what you decide to do and become.

For me, I had so much "success" that I began to lose sight of what it was that I wanted to do and what was right for me. When dealing with college, there are going to be moments when you don't know what to do next. There might be times when you look to the left and right and see that everyone is succeeding but you. It isn't about the person to your right or left—it's about you. During your time in college, get about the business of living your best life, for you. Understand that your race is your own and your story is your own, and that alone is your power. No one is you-er than you. You cannot get distracted by the successes of those around you. While you are in college just run your race and run it fiercely.

When a sprinter is running the track, he must take all of his energy to focus on the path ahead. He can't concern himself with how far away or near his competitors are. By looking behind him or beside him he is expending energy that could cost him his race.

This same idea applies to the race of college.

When you're reaching for success, just focus on what you want to do and who you want to be. Run your race. Don't compare or compete with those around you. Comparing yourself to others is a waste of the person you are.

As I write these very words, I am a Morehouse graduate. I finished. I earned my bachelor of arts degree last May, and I plan to enroll in Boston in less than thirty days. This journey I'm on feels so on-purpose and meant to be. Words are inadequate to describe how I feel going into this next chapter. I'm so pumped to go to graduate school and earn my master's. As I get closer to the start date, my excitement only grows. You, too, can experience this level of bliss, but only if you focus on yourself and give your race your all.

I don't think that I would have applied to graduate school and started working on my journey if I was still focusing on everyone else. It wasn't until I started doing things on my terms and following my path that I made this decision. Focusing on myself was the best decision I have ever made.

College is tough. It doesn't get easier, only more challenging. But luckily, with time, you'll get stronger. You will see the overarching story of your experience in college. You'll look back at your chapter one, and see how it all worked out in your favor.

As you deal with this thing called college,

Peace & Love

WAYS TO DEAL

When You Find Yourself Comparing Yourself to Others

- Don't

When Someone Gives You Advice For a Potential Next Move

- Be open-minded; you never know how life will speak to you
  - Properly assess the advice you have been given to see if it is a potential move.
  - Whenever presented with a possible situation, measure it on a scale of 1–10 and don't allow yourself to say 7. If you give the opportunity an 8 or above, jump on it.

When Applying to Graduate School

- Ask for fee waivers
- When writing your application essays think of what your potential graduate program mission is and articulate in your essays how you can be a part of that mission
- Reach out to admissions recruiters on LinkedIn and let them know you are interested in the school

FINAL DOS AND DON'TS

Dear Reader,

If you made it to this section of the book, congrats! The fact that you have read this book is evidence that you are ready for college because you finish what you start. College is such a rich experience and it has so much to offer. I'd like to conclude this book with some final dos and don'ts that I know will help you during your time in college. These actions are more objective and don't require a long story to assist the principles. These are things I wish all students understood when starting college.

Do	Don't
Go to class. Just go, you paid for it.	Skip class for any reason that isn't an emergency.
Practice safe and consensual sex while in school.	Force yourself onto anyone. Consult with your school's office of conduct if you don't understand consent and gender-based violence.
Check out your school's health center regularly for check-ups, sex education and free condoms.	Get sick and neglect getting help.

Go to parties. It's a great way to socialize and meet people.	If you are going to drink at an event, never mix dark liquors and light liquors. Your stomach will thank you.
Dance every chance you get because sometimes it's just good to dance.	Resist the urge to bust a move at a party or function.
Take time to journal and reflect on all that is happening to you.	Get so whipped away into college that you forget to be present in each moment.
Go off your campus and explore the city if it is new to you.	Don't get so caught up in your campus that you forget there is a world outside of your institution.
Your best to be nice to people.	Be a jerk.
Call your family and friends back home.	Think just because you went to college that you are better than anyone who didn't. Remain humble.
Share your adventures and lessons that you learn in college with others.	Be selfish with wisdom and knowledge—share it.
Read lots of books while in school.	Spend all your time having fun and forget to learn.
Your best to live it up. College is short and will present you with some of the best memories ever.	Die.

ACKNOWLEDGMENTS

First, I must thank the subjects of each chapter for being part of my journey and story. Thank you so much for the life lessons you taught me. I pray that our experiences documented in this book will inspire lots of readers. To Brad Pauquette, Emily Hitchcock, and the team at Columbus Publishing Lab, thank you for your dedication to this book. You are always in my corner willing to help, guide, and assist, and without you, I wouldn't be a published author.

To Michael McDonald, who inspired me to write this book in this form. After reviewing one of my blogs on my website you said I should write a cohesive body of work to help college students. I hope this book makes you proud.

I owe particular gratitude to Natalie Coles. The first speaking engagement I ever had was through you for The United Negro College Fund. It was this support from you and Elaine Davis that allowed me to realize my gift of telling good stories. I hope my professional journey will always make you proud. The adventures are not over!

To Chelsea Carson and Bob Wilson, who wrote my letters of

recommendation to Morehouse after they deferred me the first time I applied. Because of your support I was not only able to attend Morehouse, but graduate and write a book about it.

To Russell Pointer Jr., who was the first Morehouse student I ever met. Thank you for your support, wisdom, and guidance.

To all of my professors at Morehouse who guided me along my academic path.

To Cathy Tyler, Kara Walker, Synera Shelton and Chimere Stanford Jefferson. You ladies were my family when I was away from Ohio. Thank you for always allowing me to crash lunch meetings and vent in your offices, and thank you for encouraging me throughout my time at Morehouse.

To Cornell Young, who has been the epitome of what Morehouse brotherhood should be. You were the first person I asked to review my table of contents and book cover. Thank you for your incredible friendship and early support.

To Keon McKay for capturing the very essence of my vision for the book cover with your exquisite photography.

To my family whom I love deeply, ET and Monica Sumlin, my loving parents, and my siblings Orlando, William, and Britney Sumlin.

To my bro squad, Corbin Sanders, Sean Sheppheard, Eugene Jamil Malik Rashid Muhammad and John Eagan. They say college is where you make your friends for life, and I can say with confidence that this is the truth. You all made my experience at Morehouse incredible. I hugely credit all of my success to you guys for your unwavering support, camaraderie, and help up the dorm room stairs after parties (hahaha). I love you guys.

I will conclude by shouting out some of my favorite authors whose work inspires me to write better: Tim Ferriss, Brené Brown, Gabrielle Bernstein and Oprah. Each of you and your work inspires me deeply. Hopefully one day we get to work together to inspire the world.

ABOUT THE AUTHOR

On January 7 in Dayton, Ohio, Christopher Michael Sumlin was born destined for greatness. He comes from a tight-knit Christian family and is the second oldest of four children. His father was a minister and church was the basis of Chris' young adult life. At age fourteen, Chris attended a high school called The Charles School at Ohio Dominican University in Columbus, Ohio. With the love and support of family and mentors, Chris graduated from the school in five years, earning both his high school diploma and an associate of arts degree from Ohio Dominican University.

Chris recently graduated from the historic Morehouse College in Atlanta, Georgia, majoring in cinema, television and emerging media studies. Chris hopes to one day be a television producer who creates family-friendly, inspiring television. In the summer of 2015, Chris interned at both Fox Studios and the BET Awards in Los Angeles, California. During his stint in Los Angeles, Chris spent a lot of time alone reflecting and learning about life. His adventures inspired him to write his debut book, *Dealing with This Thing Called Life*, which was released in April 2016. This book is available wherever books are sold.

Chris currently attends Boston University where he is pursuing a master of science degree in television producing and management. He will graduate in January of 2019.